Urban Schools, Public Will

Urban Schools, Public Will

MAKING EDUCATION WORK FOR ALL OUR CHILDREN

Norm Fruchter

Foreword by Theresa Perry

Teachers College, Columbia University
New York and London

Published by Teachers College Press, 1234 Amsterdam Avenue, New York, NY 10027

Library of Congress Cataloging-in-Publication Data

Fruchter, Norm, 1937-
  Urban schools, public will : making education work for all our children
Fruchter.
      p. cm.
  Includes bibliographical references and index.
    ISBN-13: 978-0-8077-4740-7 (pbk : alk. paper)
    ISBN-13: 978-0-8077-4741-4 (cloth : alk. paper)
    ISBN-10: 0-8077-4740-8 (pbk : alk. paper)
    ISBN-10: 0-8077-4741-6 (cloth : alk. paper)
  1. Education, Urban—United States. 2. Segregation in education—United States.
3. Educational change—United States—Case studies. I. Title.
    LC5131.F78 2007
    370.9173'2
                                                              2006021906

ISBN-13:   ISBN-10:
978-0-8077-4740-7 (paper) 0-8077-4740-8 (paper)
978-0-8077-4741-4 (cloth) 0-8077-4741-6 (cloth)

Printed on acid-free paper
Manufactured in the United States of America

14 13 12 11 10 09 08 07   8 7 6 5 4 3 2 1

Contents

Foreword

WE—THAT IS, me, my friends, and my colleagues—go to meetings, with educators, give talks, and occasionally write about what it will take to transform urban schooling to educate black and Latino students for first-class citizenship. Sometimes, despite our best intentions, it is as if we were sleepwalking. We have collectively participated in so many struggles. We have strategized and made what seem like the same power plays over and over again, made similar arguments to different groups of people at different points in our lives.

It is as if we were sleepwalking because today, as perhaps never before, we are overwhelmed by the lack of clarity among progressive people—educators, elected officials, community activists, public intellectuals, black and white people—about what this struggle to transform urban schools is really about. For some, it's about saving a few black and Latino kids by getting them into charter schools; for others, it is about protecting a group of public schools from the constraints of district offices and unions. For some, it is about preparing a few students for competitive schools; for others, it is about coming up with strategies and programs to keep white people in city schools; and for still others it is about meeting the state accountability standards at the proficiency level.

We live in a time when the public discourse about improving public schools is framed in terms of markets, accountability, individual choice—where choice has replaced struggle for equal educational opportunity. We live in a time in which the transformation of urban schools is often approached and framed as a technical task, requiring only that we cobble together people who are smart enough to analyze the issues and come up with the correct solution. And then, we need only get enough of these smart people to help districts or schools to implement what they have come up with.

In the midst of this dizzying confusion, or to be more precise, in the midst of this depoliticized and ahistorical discourse about urban schooling, Norm Fruchter's book, URBAN SCHOOLS, PUBLIC WILL, lifts us out of this morass, and in a compelling, passionate, and intellectually rigorous narrative brilliantly reaffirms what this struggle to transform urban schools is all about. He effectively repositions the work to transform urban schools as fundamentally the new common school movement for urban America. The first and last chapters, the book's bookends, redefine the conversation about the transformation of urban schools.

Fruchter begins the book with a discussion of the social, political, and economic forces, the federal and state policies, and the personal decisions of white people that have created and reproduce urban America and by extension urban schools. Importantly, in his discussion it becomes clear that problematic urban schools, like urban America, are not the creations of the poor people of color who reside in cities and whose children disproportionately attend urban schools. He refuses to allow the American public to once again blame black and Latino communities for the situation they find themselves in because of structured inequality and the decisions of the power elites. He asks us to see the current condition of urban schools as a failure of the public will to fulfill the promise of *Brown*, and as a consequence, as an extension of the racially qualified form of education that has been reserved for black people since the time of slavery. Appropriately, in the last chapter, he examines the research on the burgeoning movement to use community organizing to demand that urban school systems provide excellent education for students of color. If the situation of urban schools is but the latest iteration of the racially qualified form of education of the pre–civil rights era, North and South, and if mobilization and organizing were central to the gains that have been made, then it stands to reason that organizing will also be critical in the contemporary struggle in urban America for equal educational opportunity—in the new urban common school movement.

In its focus on organizing, the book challenges us to situate the school reform movement in the historical tradition of organizing to create the demand for education. When the Freedman's Bureau decided that it could not afford to continue to fund schools in New Orleans for the formerly enslaved Africans, African Americans organized and presented petitions miles long, demanding that schools for their children be restored, even if it meant levying an additional tax on their community (Anderson, 1988). During the Civil War, black soldiers organized, demanding the books they needed to teach and learn (Williams, 2006). In 1928, the black community of Little Rock, Arkansas, protested against the establishment of an industrial high school for their children. They wanted "a real high school . . . one that would give a thorough educational training . . . and a curriculum upon which a college education could be predicated" (Anderson, 1988, p. 210). In the 1960s, African American students in Chicago went on strike, demanding a more rigorous academic program.

Avoiding rhetoric, in an exquisitely written and engaging book, Norm Fruchter asks us to see the work of transforming schools as fundamentally political work. And he shows how that work requires considerable knowledge, research, and expertise, as well as organizing, if we are to create and sustain the demand for excellent education for children of color and recalibrate power relationships in urban America.

Between the bookends, in the remaining chapters, the author effortlessly interweaves and draws on his decades of work to make schools work for poor children of color, integrating throughout issues of race, power, and white privilege. He examines the practices of those districts that have been able to raise the achievement of black and Latino students, He pores over the elements that made it possible for the Department of Defense schools to substantially reduce the achievement gap between students of color and white students, with an eye toward arguing that it is possible to create a system of schools with a culture of achievement, He convincingly takes on all of the iterations of choice, from in-district choice to the charter school movement, effectively demonstrating the limitations of choice as an organizing principle for the reform of urban schools and convincingly putting to rest the claim that choice is the next stage in the civil rights movement. He lays out why it is important that accountability be coupled with sustained work in schools in order to help educators develop the capacity to meet the standards. He shows how schools fail to develop cultures that respond to black and Latino students.

This is a hopeful book, because the author writes out of a life of struggle to make schools work for the disenfranchised, marginalized, and oppressed. It is a hopeful book because the author lives, works, researches, and organizes in the city. This book is not about "other people's children." It is apparent on every page that Norm Fruchter believes that the struggle to transform urban schools is about him, about all of us, as much as it is about the parents of the children currently attending schools in urban America.

Theresa Perry
Simmons College

REFERENCES

Anderson, J. D. (1988). *The education of Blacks in the South, 1860–1935*. Chapel Hill: University of North Carolina Press.

Willams, H. E. (2005). *Self-taught: African American education in slavery and freedom*. Chapel Hill: University of North Carolina Press.

Acknowledgments

THIS BOOK has evolved from a decade-long dialogue with my colleagues in the Community Involvement Program of New York University's Institute for Education and Social Policy, which I directed from 1995 to 2006. Our program set out to engage and support community-based organizations in local school improvement and district-wide reform in New York City, and to research such efforts in other cities across the country. Kavitha Mediratta, Eric Zachary, Richard Gray, Barbara Gross, Deinya Phenix, Mili Bonilla, Edwina Branch-Smith, Seema Shah, Amy Cohen, Megan Hester, Lamson Lam, Sara McAlister, and Cindy Maguire shared their work, their reflections, and their dilemmas with me; what we've learned informs the core of this book. I owe a particular debt to Kavitha's and Eric's efforts to define the strategic components of the Community Involvement Program's groundbreaking work, and to Kavitha for a very useful critical reading of my treatment of organizing and social capital formation.

I am grateful to other Institute colleagues as well. Carol Ascher and I have sustained a discussion about how best to assess school reform efforts for almost a decade. Her review of our Institute's charter school analyses, as well as her reading of my arguments about what organizing can accomplish, provided several useful revisions. Dana Lockwood, the Institute's director of two major evaluations of school reform efforts, taught me much about the combination of painstaking analysis and humility essential to effective evaluation. Dorothy Siegel, a colleague on my Brooklyn school board as well as at the Institute, enriched my understanding of how school and district structures and processes so often fail to meet the particular and diverse needs of urban students. Amy Ellen Schwartz and Leanna Stiefel, professors at NYU's Wagner School, educated me about the potential and complexities of quantitative analysis, as did Colin Chellman, Meryle Weinstein, Hella Bel Hadj Amor, and Tom Saunders, colleagues at the Institute. I am especially grateful to Sara McAlister, a research assistant at the Institute, for her help in reviewing and editing my sources and references. Without the assistance, support, and friendship of Gerri Pompey, the Institute's administrator, not only this book, but my working life would have been considerably impoverished.

This book also developed from an education policy course I co-taught for 10 years with Robert Berne, Vice President for Health at NYU. Planning and annually revising the course with Bob created an evolving discussion about how public education might be improved, which is reflected in all the issues this book engages.

Many friends read drafts of this work and contributed useful revisions and suggestions. Anne Henderson, with whom I've discussed issues of parent and citizen participation in school improvement for many years, offered sage and perceptive comments throughout the manuscript, as did Herb Kohl, Gordon Pradl, Walter Stafford, and Dan Challener. I have had long discussions with Ann Bastian about the issues this book explores, and she made particularly helpful suggestions as to how to frame the theme of the nation's refusal to integrate and the consequences of that refusal. Dick Booth, an English colleague and a friend, gave me specific revisions and judicious advice that immeasurably improved my treatment of the English inspectorate. Michael Rustin's paper on inspection and audit contributed enormously to my framing of accountability, and I have benefited from many conversations with him across our half-century of friendship.

Jesse Register, Bill Kennedy, and Dan Challener reviewed the section about the work and accomplishments of the Hamilton County (Chattanooga) school district, and gave me very useful feedback. I have worked with all three for almost a decade, and am grateful for how generously they have shared their work and their insights about how schools and districts can be improved. Jim Connell did the same for the work of First Things First in Kansas City, and Helaine Doran reviewed my analysis of District 2's improvement strategies and provided a very useful critical lens. My daughter, Chenda, and my son, Lev, read several chapters, and my son contributed several insights from the perspective of a New York City public high school teacher. I am grateful to all of them.

Amy Rosenberg, my editor at Teachers College Press, provided advice throughout the manuscript about how to achieve the crispness, clarity, and compression I wanted; she was a model of editorial assistance.

My wife, Heather Lewis, read and reread the manuscript and offered comments, revisions, and advice about reframing issues and arguments that vastly improved each chapter. Her historian's insights and perspectives, and her experience as a school reformer, have contributed immensely to how I think about the intersections of race, ethnicity, class, and public education reform. Without her support, companionship, and love, this book would not have been written.

Introduction

I never met a white person till I was a grown man. I never went to school with a white till I was twenty-six years old, at Harvard Law School. The insult of segregation was searing and unforgettable. It has left a great scar, and will be with me for the rest of my life. It causes you in terror to form reflexes of protection. It's unnatural but necessary. So I decided a long time ago to join the social justice movement. It was salvaging. We all have to die, and I preferred to have just one death. It seems to me that to suffer insult without response is to die many deaths.
　　　　　　　　　—Randall Robinson, "Randall Robinson Interview"

THIS BOOK IS about race and education. It proposes two critical arguments: that the nation's urban public schools can be transformed to effectively educate their poor students of color, and that the nation's urban school districts are the key agents of this transformation. To support these arguments, in this book I explore how the nation's public will has imposed failing schools on students of color and then blamed those students for the resulting achievement gap.

I begin this exploration in the book's initial chapter by deconstructing a relatively new but invidious myth—that U.S. public education is so ineffective that it must be transformed by market solutions. I argue that this myth of universal public school inadequacy is a defensive reaction to a real failure—the national refusal to implement the Supreme Court's *Brown* mandate to integrate our public schools. Although the nation celebrated the *Brown* decision as a triumph of American democracy in the Cold War setting of the 1950s, it resolutely refused to implement the mandate across the ensuing half century. What has resulted are urban schools more segregated than when *Brown* was litigated, and a race-based achievement gap that dooms millions of poor students of color to inadequate education and limited futures.

In Chapter 1, I analyze how the partisans of privatization have transformed the failure to integrate our schools into a condemnation of all the nation's public schooling. I then develop an example—the nation's military schooling—of public school effectiveness in closing the resulting race-based achievement gap. Finally, I argue that the culture of American schooling can be transformed to effectively educate students of color, if sufficient public will can be mobilized.

In Chapter 2 I examine how changing the culture of schooling can reduce the achievement gap. I offer a close analysis of two memoirs of African American youth, to emphasize the limitations of formal schooling in their education and development. I examine the research and the resulting proposals of several African American scholars for how to transform the culture of schooling to effectively educate students of color.

Chapter 3 concerns issues of accountability; in it, I introduce the second of the book's central arguments: that the role of the school district is critical to reducing the achievement gap and improving student academic outcomes. I distinguish the accountability functions of audit—setting standards and assessing student, school and district outcomes—from the accountability functions of inspection, analyzing what schools need to do to improve those outcomes and providing the necessary supports. I conclude the chapter by assessing the shortcomings of the No Child Left Behind Act from the perspectives of audit and inspection.

In Chapter 4, I explore the limitations of choice as a panacea for the failures of schooling. I analyze the arguments of key choice proponents and then examine the trajectory of outcomes in New York City's District 4, once the epitome of a successful choice initiative.[1] I also establish the critical supports that both choice initiatives and charter schools require, and define those supports as functions that restructured school districts can provide.

I extend this argument about the critical role of the school district in Chapter 5 by examining how three urban districts—New York City's District 2; Kansas City, Kansas; and Hamilton County (Chattanooga), Tennessee—improved their students' achievement and reduced their race-based achievement gaps.

In the final chapter, Chapter 6, I explore how the national failure of public will to improve urban public schools can be effectively challenged, through community-based organizing for school reform. I analyze the campaigns of grassroots groups, many affiliated with national organizing networks, to improve their local schools and districts. I examine the strategies and outcomes of such education organizing and link those organizing efforts to improving neighborhood social capital and increasing neighborhood participation in democratic action.

Throughout the book I introduce vignettes from my education experience to illustrate the issues that each chapter covers. My experience with public schooling has been quite broad: I have been a public school teacher, a parent organizer, a PTA president and a school board member, a foundation education grant-maker, and an evaluator and researcher. I began teaching in a London day-release college, akin to a U.S. alternative high school, in my early twenties, as a way to support myself while I wrote a novel, and helped to edit a small New Left journal. I learned about organizing as a member of the Newark, New Jersey, community-organizing project of Students for a Democratic Society. I became a high school teacher in New York City and eventually codirected an alternative high school for dropouts in the Ironbound section of Newark, with colleagues from the Newark organizing project. After I left the Newark high school, I helped to organize a baccalaureate program for community activists and public-sector workers at a Jesuit college in Jersey City, New Jersey. Simultaneously I returned to organizing, working with parents to improve their local schools in a number of New Jersey cities. Once my children entered public school in my Brooklyn neighborhood, I served on several PTAs and then successfully ran for my community school board, serving for 10 years as a board member and an officer.

At the beginning of my tenure on the school board, I worked for a national education nonprofit, conducting evaluations of foundation-funded school reform efforts. During my later years on the board, I served as the education grant-maker for a large New York City foundation that supported new small high schools, school restructuring, and other reform efforts throughout the New York City public school system. Across the past decade, I directed the New York University Institute for Education and Social Policy, whose large-scale research studies of national and local school reform efforts were complemented by the efforts of its Community Involvement Program to help neighborhood-based organizations improve their local schools. From these varied experiences, I have constructed the vignettes, which I hope will illuminate and crystallize the arguments of each chapter.

Whenever aspiring graduate students ask me to describe my education career, I joke that it has been, at best, spotty. That's my way of caricaturing its unplanned and apparently erratic nature. Although all my choices were inadvertent, in hindsight I can discern a pattern. I have been engaged in a long march through public education in an effort to understand how that institution, so critical to the formation of consciousness and the reproduction of our society, might be transformed to reduce its prevailing inequities. Those "savage inequalities," in Jonathan Kozol's phrase, so limit the provision of schooling, particularly to poor students of color, that they have warped the capacity of education to produce what Amy Guttman calls "conscious social reproduction" and the possibility of a just society. How we do schooling in this country, just as how we do housing, health care, the distribution of wealth and income, and the provision of justice, is fundamentally inequitable and unjust. This book is a small effort to contribute to more equitable and effective education and a more equitable and just society.

A word about usage: Throughout this book I use *children of color*, or *students of color*, to refer to all those young people treated differently, and inequitably, by the pervasive practices of public education's institutional racism. I have minimized the use of the term *minority*, primarily because it has a tendency to marginalize its subjects. Moreover, in many urban districts, children of color are the overwhelming majority of the public school population, while white students are often a quite small minority. Moreover, perhaps by midcentury, students of color will eventually comprise the majority of public school students in the entire nation.

But my usage conflates key distinctions. This book focuses primarily on how our nation's inequitable schooling affects African American students and how those limiting effects might be overcome. I have not specifically addressed how schooling inequities play out in the education of Latino and Asian students and how their education might be transformed as well.

This limitation risks narrowing my arguments. As Gilberto Conchas observes, using a black-white dichotomy to examine educational inequity "distorts the experiences of other racial minority groups [and] the intricacy of between- and within-group variation is lost" (2006, p. 9). My defense for focusing primarily on African American students is that the target of my analysis is the systemic structures that produce schooling inequality and how those structures might be transformed. Although those discriminatory structures operate across our society's racial and ethnic divisions, they are often starker within the African American schooling experience. Thus for the sake of clarity of analysis, I have narrowed the lens of my examination.

In Chapter 2, for example, I analyze two accounts of the coming-of-age experience of two African American males and examine the proposals of several African American scholars for how the culture of schooling can be transformed to produce high achievement by African American students. An expanding field of scholarship is examining the effects of schooling inequity on a wide range of students from Latino and Asian backgrounds, as well as African Americans, and analyzing how those students are able to overcome the discriminatory structure of schooling and achieve academic success (Carter, 2005; Darder & Torres, 2004; Gandara, 1995; Kao & Tienda, 1998; Lee, 1996; Noguera, 2003; Romo & Falbo, 1996; Stanton-Salazar, 2001; Suarez-Orosco & Suarez-Orosco, 2001; Valenzuela, 1999). The work of these and other scholars is contributing to an enriching analysis of how students from a variety of racial and ethnic backgrounds can transcend the institutional limits of inequitable schooling. Hopefully this book's arguments will contribute to a greater understanding of how structured inequality in public schooling affects all children of color and how those discriminatory structures can be overcome.

The Failure of *Brown* and the Degradation of Urban Schools

From the *Brown v. Board* decision 50 years ago to the present, few have challenged the notion that opportunity should be made more equitable, but many have argued about what that actually meant. The theory of equality of opportunity fit with our conception of American democracy or what Gunnar Myrdal, writing in his book *An American Dilemma* termed the "American creed." The practice of it, however, has hit a brick wall—the divide between the privileged and the non-privileged in America.
—Patricia Graham, "Whom Should Our Schools Serve?"

E ACH SEMESTER when I begin a course on education policy, I ask my graduate students to try the following thought experiment. Think about your great-grandparents and your grandparents, I tell them. Consider what you know about where they grew up and how they lived. Then give me your best guess about whether your great-grandparents' schooling was better or worse than the schooling your grandparents received. My students quickly decide that the education their grandparents received was superior to their great-grandparents'. Next I ask them to compare the schooling their grandparents and parents received. Again my classes decide that their parents' education was the better. When I ask them to compare their parents' education to the schooling they themselves experienced, the responses are similar. Overwhelmingly my students agree that their education was better than their parents'. Then I ask them to consider their own education compared to the education they think their children will receive.

Responses to this final question change the pattern dramatically. Usually more than half the class decides that the education their children have received or will receive is not, or will not be, as good as their own. I challenge my students to consider why the pattern of historical progress in education they deduced from their predecessors' experience has ended with them. Then I explain that I introduced the experiment to highlight how significantly perceptions of public education's effectiveness have changed across the decades since the mandate of *Brown v. Board of Education* has yielded to resegregation.

THWARTING THE PROMISE OF *BROWN*

A half century after *Brown v. Board of Education* was decided by a unanimous Supreme Court, the nation's schools are more segregated than they were in 1954, when the case was decided. The resurgence of segregated schooling has ended the hope that *Brown* would dismantle the stratified nature of American public education. After decades of conflict about whether to implement the equal access to education that the *Brown* court envisioned, the nation's public will and a conservative Supreme Court have accomplished the resegregation of our public schools. What we currently strive for is quality education rather than integrated education. And we define quality education as the improvement in standardized-test scores and the narrowing of the test score gap between white students and students of color, no matter how segregated the schools they attend.

It is difficult, in this climate, to remember the unbridled optimism with which many partisans of integrated schooling celebrated the *Brown* decision. An example was recently recounted by Cass Sunstein, one of the nation's foremost legal scholars. "Thurgood Marshall," Sunstein recalled, "predicted that school segregation would be entirely stamped out within five years" (2004, p. 102) after the *Brown* decision.

How *Brown* became the vision for a more equitable system of American public education is a fascinating story that several scholars have recounted (see Klarman, 2004; Kluger, 1975). This chapter will not retell that story. My aim, instead, is to unpack one symptom of the bad faith that structures our nation's racial beliefs—the notion that public schooling is failing our students. My argument is that this notion is a myth, propagated to reduce the discomfort that has accompanied our failure to institutionalize the integrated schooling that the *Brown* decision demanded.

The reality of our public school failure is not universal but specific, historically rooted, and ongoing. As a nation we have always failed to effectively educate poor students of color. For the three decades after slavery was officially ended, through the ensuing half century from *Plessy v. Ferguson* to *Brown*, we have ignored, tolerated, dismissed, or deflected our failure to provide the equality of education to children of color that should accompany "liberty and justice for all." The *Brown* decision challenged that failure but did not succeed in changing it. As Gloria Ladson-Billings (2004) argues:

> *Brown* is more accurately characterized as a first step in a long, arduous process to rid the nation of its most pernicious demons—racism and White supremacy. While we celebrate its potential, we must be clear about its limitations. The nation has never fully and honestly dealt with its "race" problem. Our lack of historical understanding seems to obliterate some rather daunting facts. For example, slavery existed legally in North America for almost 250 years. An apartheid-like social segregation was legally sanctioned for another hundred years. The United States as a nation is but 228 years old and existed as a slave nation longer than it has existed as a free one. The norms, customs, mores, and folkways that surround our racial ecology are not easily cast aside. Our attempt to deal with racial problems through our schools is an incomplete strategy. (p. 10)

The *Brown* decision ended the charade of separate-but-equal education and challenged the nation to transform its segregated public schooling to realize the Supreme Court's vision of equality of education. Instead, in school districts throughout the nation, citizens fought against the Supreme Court's mandate through a variety of legal strategies; public protest; and, too often, open racist violence. Currently, as studies by the Harvard University Civil Rights Project have demonstrated, our nation's public schools are more than 40% students of color, and most of those students attend schools that are quite segregated (Orfield & Lee, 2005). The project's research also indicates that levels of segregation for black and Latino students have risen steadily across the past few decades, and the nation's high school drop-out rate is concentrated in inner-city schools serving students of color. Ultimately, as a nation, we have not only maintained segregated public schools, we have actually intensified educational segregation and schooling stratification by race and class.

Our refusal to integrate our schools, and our acceptance of segregated schooling, has exacerbated the contradiction at the core of our nation's response to the mandate of *Brown*—we celebrated the judgment, but we refused to carry it out. The discomfort this contradiction generates has intensified as our commitment to segregation continues to impose failing schools and inadequate education on students of color. To contain this discomfort, we increasingly treat urban public schools as if they had created their segregated and inadequate conditions and were solely responsible for the national failure to effectively educate poor students of color. The past decade has introduced a new dimension to this transformation of discomfort into blame. The indictment of urban systems' failure to effectively educate poor students of color has metamorphosed into a condemnation of all American public education and an embrace of market remedies as the necessary cure.

To set out the argument in such bare outline is to risk assigning causality to the interplay of large-scale societal processes such as deindustrialization, suburbanization, and the hollowing out of urban core areas. As Jack M. Balkin (2001) argues in a review of the Supreme Court decisions that limited the scope of desegregation orders and then restricted and ultimately relaxed their power, current segregation "is the result of a complicated mix of social, political, legal and economic factors, rather than the result of direct state commands ordering racial separation" (p. 7). The mix of factors, for example, that has isolated poor families of color in the decaying cores of urban centers, and produced inadequate school systems serving those families' children, includes the following:

- Globalization, the consequent dispersion of industry, and the disappearance of manufacturing jobs once located in urban centers
- The growth of suburbs, fueled by federally subsidized mortgages granted overwhelmingly to white families, and the development of superhighways and ring roads subsidized by federal highway funds, which supported the abandonment of central cities by middle-class and working-class families
- The regressive state education funding policies and constrained local tax bases that are increasingly unable to support appropriate education in urban areas

These factors combined with a fierce resistance to integration to produce affluent suburbs and impoverished cities with poor families of color anchoring their core populations. The desperate plight of poor black families in New Orleans after the flooding that followed Hurricane Katrina in August 2005 is the most dramatic recent demonstration of the cost of the resegregation, economic marginalization, and political disenfranchisement that our nation has imposed on poor inner-city families. As Mark Naison, director of Fordham University's urban studies program observed after the Hurricane Katrina devastation, "Is this what the pioneers of the civil rights movement fought to achieve, a society where many black people are as trapped and isolated by their poverty as they were by legal segregation laws?" (cited in DeParle, 2005, p. 4)

During the 1970s I codirected an alternative high school for dropouts in one of the immigrant enclaves in Newark, New Jersey. Our approximately 100 students were a mix of African Americans, Latinos, and ethnic whites. Because the high school was funded as an experiment in juvenile delinquency prevention, our students' common denominators were a failure to complete high school and at least one arrest on their juvenile records. We were quite successful in reducing recidivism, one of the school's core goals, but that is not the point of this vignette.

During the years in which I worked at the Newark high school, the city was recovering from decades of economic decline and the uprisings of the late 1960s. Its politics were in transition from traditional white ethnic Democratic Party control to the dominance of the city's African American majority. The city's first black mayor had recently been elected and was consolidating a reform-minded economic-development regime. Indeed, it was the new African American chief of police who suggested that our fledgling school might qualify for a federal delinquency prevention grant.

During my years at the high school, my parents retired to Florida and I made frequent trips to visit them. They befriended several retired families who had run businesses—restaurants, drug stores, supermarkets, and printing establishments—in downtown Newark. Whenever we met, I made no secret of my job in Newark and often explained that I spent every workday in the city and hours each week downtown at the board of education, the police department, and the varieties of businesses that supplied our school's needs. Yet my parents' friends regaled me with stories about how bad conditions had become in Newark, how their businesses in particular and Newark's downtown in general had been ruined by "them." Eventually I stopped protesting about how thoroughly my own experience belied their convictions, because they literally ignored everything I said. I decided that the depth of their belief in the ruination of Newark was more than an *idée fixe*. Leaving Newark seemed to have generated powerful internal mechanisms that drove them to constantly denigrate the city they had left behind.

A cumulative national response to the forces that have shaped our suburbs and reshaped our cities has intersected with a half century of struggle over the *Brown* mandate to create an indictment of urban public schooling, and then a condemnation of all public schooling, analogous to the mechanisms that impelled my parents' friends to portray Newark as a disaster zone.

After rejecting the choice to implement *Brown*, and instead intensifying the stratification of American public education, the nation has turned on the beleaguered urban schools that those choices created and blamed them for their failure to achieve the aspirations of integration. The forces of opposition to *Brown* have indicted the urban school systems that bore the brunt of the nation's renewed commitment to segregation, and transformed those systems' specific failure to educate students of color into a wholesale accusation of the failure of American public education.

THE FORCES OF OPPOSITION TO *BROWN*

I was a sophomore in college, part of a literary clique besotted with the American giants—Hemingway, Fitzgerald, Faulkner—who dominated 20th-century modernist fiction. Partisans of integration and inspired by the Supreme Court's *Brown* decision, we were both appalled and fascinated by William Faulkner's "A Letter to the North," published in *Life* magazine in March 1956. In his letter, Faulkner portrays himself as a moderate who has absorbed considerable criticism in his defense of integration. He pleads with northerners to slow the pace of integration, to give the South time to adjust to this new historical reality. And he also hints at the violence to come if the North cannot heed his plea. "To all Southerners," Faulkner argues, "no matter which side of the question of racial equality they supported, the first implication, and, to the Southerner—even promise, of force and violence was the Supreme Court decision itself" (p. 51).

Faulkner cautions northerners that if they press integration too quickly and too rigorously, southern moderates like himself will be forced into the camp of the extremists. What still motivates the South, Faulkner argues, is what motivated it to fight the Civil War almost 100 years ago. "What that war should have done, but failed to do, was to prove to the North that the South will go to any length, even that fatal and already doomed one, before it will accept alteration of its racial condition by mere force of the law or economic threat" (p. 52).

Faulkner's warnings were accurate; consider the battles that characterized the first-stage southern resistance to integration. Governors, legislatures, and mayors in several states pledged armed opposition to the Supreme Court's mandate. After Arkansas governor Orval Faubus used the state's National Guard to deny nine African American students entrance to Little Rock's Central High School in 1957, President Dwight D. Eisenhower was forced to order the 101st Airborne Division to escort the students into the school.

In addition to this overt level of resistance, southern states, counties, and cities used legal means to subvert the integration decree. Prince Edward County in Virginia, one of the original school districts involved in *Brown*, closed its public school system for 5 years and helped establish private academies that enrolled only white students. Virginia recently established a $5,500 annual scholarship program for state residents denied an education because of the state's refusal to intervene in counties like Prince Edward, as well as by the state's creation of a voucher program to help white children enroll in private schools as part of its commitment to "massive resistance" to desegregation (Janofsky, 2005, p. 1). In other southern jurisdictions, the formation of private schools and Christian academies drew substantial percentages of white students from local public school systems and contributed to the resegregation and severe underfunding of those systems.

Ironically, in terms of Faulkner's warning, some of the most polarizing conflicts exploded outside the South. Integration orders, particularly those mandating the busing of African American students to predominantly white schools, led to massive resistance and sometimes overt violence, most dramatically in Boston, Chicago, and Los Angeles. One of the most polarized, though violence-free, struggles was waged in Richmond, California, across the bay from San Francisco, chronicled by Lillian B. Rubin in *Busing and Backlash: White Against White in a California School District* (1972).

The story that Rubin (1972) narrates is familiar. The newly elected liberal school board of the unified Richmond district vacillates about integration, caught between the demands for integrated schooling from a vocal black minority and the increasingly angry responses of white middle- and working-class constituents. To assuage the tide of conservative opposition, the board denies any intention to bus students, but refuses to say how it will carry out its commitment to integration. Instead, the board appoints a commission to study the situation and recommend a plan.

The growing white opposition uses the public hearings about the plan as a springboard for organizing. First, the opposition defeats a tax increase critical to restoring the district's imperiled finances. Then the opposition elects two integration opponents to the board. Finally, in 1969, the opposition captures the board completely. As its first action, the new board not only guarantees no busing but also reverses the previous board's commitments to desegregation. It subsequently implements a very limited voluntary open-enrollment program, restricts citizen participation in district policy deliberations, and imposes strict censorship on the district's schools.

Rubin's (1972) signal contribution is to situate this narrative in a political context in which liberals are as responsible as conservatives for the failure to desegregate. Liberal governance of the previous Richmond district had created segregated schooling for the district's substantial minority of black students. This racially separate schooling followed the development of segregated housing during World War II, when the establishment of Kaiser shipyards brought thousands of white and black workers from the South and Southwest into the eastern bay area. As one of Rubin's interviewee's describes it:

> "My family brought me here when I was two when they came to work in the shipyards. I lived in Harbor Gate; y'know, the white housing project for shipyard workers. I just don't understand. When the federal government brought us up here and built those houses, they built one tract for whites

and one for blacks. They built the segregated housing, and then they come along a few years later and call us racists." (p. 77)

Busing became one of the key mechanisms for maintaining school-ing segregation throughout the eastern bay area. Both black and white students were bused past their neighborhood schools before unification, and the practice was intensified after unification to protect the newly unified white suburban districts from receiving black students.

The newly elected white pro-integration school board of the Richmond Unified School District (RUSD) was primarily composed of "an educated, sophisticated, cosmopolitan, upper-middle-class elite; moderates by both temperament and social position who were supported by many who would soon become their enemies" (p. 85). Their governing style was, in Rubin's analysis, a traditional mix of noblesse oblige, paternalism, and what Rubin, using a definition first suggested by Herbert Gans (1967) in *The Levittowners*, defines as performance politics, the rituals of deliberation that cloak the reality that the key decisions have already been made.

Rubin (1972) argues that the growing white opposition to desegrega-tion, combined with the growing black demands for integration, over-whelmed the capacity of the liberal board to govern by the usual mechanisms of elite democratic rule. Had the liberal board been fully committed to the necessity for integration, Rubin suggests, they could have pushed through an integration program and hoped that Richmond's diverse constituencies would have ultimately accepted it. The resulting integration policy might well have become part of the necessary response to the new order the *Brown* ruling had established.

Rubin uses Reginald G. Damerell's *Triumph in a White Suburb* (1968) to provide an example of a school board (in Teaneck, New Jersey) that used this scenario effectively and exposed the racism implicit in the opposition. She also cites the success of other school boards, particularly Charlotte-Mecklenburg, North Carolina, in carrying out court-ordered desegregation. But the RUSD board did not have the capacity to act similarly. "For the lib-eral board members to have acted so forthrightly would have required an unambivalent commitment to integration, a supportive liberal constituency, and the political philosophy to support such firm action. The liberal board had none of these" (Rubin, 1972, p. 96).

The school board's inability to govern decisively, in an increasingly polarized political situation, led to a pattern of indecision that provoked an increasingly organized white conservative opposition to oust the board and terminate the possibility of desegregation. (No violence occurred in Richmond throughout this struggle except an interracial fight between Richmond High School students.) Rubin's analysis also indicates a significant white student enrollment decrease in the RUSD from 1966 to 1970, an early indication of what would become a more substantial movement of white families out of the district in the following decade.

THE FLIGHT FROM CITIES

Many northern, midwestern, and western cities experienced variants of the conflicts that almost paralyzed Richmond. The threat of integrated schooling, combined with the processes of industrial dispersion, suburban housing development, and highway construction influenced millions of white middle- and working-class families to leave central cities for the neighboring suburbs. Low-cost mortgages, subsidized by the federal government but made available almost entirely to white families only, helped spark this movement. In many cities, blockbusting by the same consortia of realtors that had maintained white-only neighborhoods also helped to swell the exodus and turn the core neighborhoods of central cities into all-black districts.

My family experienced the effects of blockbusting when I was in high school. I was born and raised in Camden, New Jersey; my parents worked across the Delaware River in Philadelphia. My mother was a bookkeeper for a women's dress manufacturing firm that was sold, and subsequently failed to survive overseas competition, during the 1960s. My father worked on the assembly line for a series of major electronic companies that relocated to the suburbs or moved abroad during the 1950s. When my parents bought their first home in Camden in 1944, their neighborhood was almost completely white, with a few African American families amid the primarily Italian, Irish, and Polish residents. Eleven years later, when I was in my last year of high school, white families from our neighborhood began moving to the near suburbs, fueled by rumors of black incursions and encouraged, if not panicked, by concerted realtor blockbusting.

I remember my parents sitting at their dining-room table staring at a spread of realtors' leaflets urging homeowners to sell quickly before housing values deteriorated as the "Negro invasion" accelerated. My father, who hated change, was very reluctant to move. My mother was convinced they would lose their housing equity if they waited too long to sell and the neighborhood "tipped." My parents sold their house in the spring of 1955 for what they had paid for it a decade before. They moved to an overwhelmingly white high-rise condominium complex about five miles away. The complex housed restaurants, a dry-cleaning establishment, a beauty parlor, and a supermarket and offered an express bus to downtown Philadelphia.

I have visited Camden throughout the subsequent years; the city was so leeched by white flight and the exodus of industry that it has become one of the nation's poorest cities. My Camden High School class reunions are held in motel ballrooms in nearby suburbs, because the organizers fear that few graduates are prepared to return to center-city venues.

The resegregation of American public schools resulted from millions of individual family decisions like the one my parents made about where to live; where and when to move; whom to sell to; and above all, where to send the children to school. Such intensely personal familial choices are made within large-scale economic, political, and social policies that constitute the warp and weft of the neighborhood, community and urban/suburban segregation that sustains the continuing stratification of American public schooling.

As a nation with a proud tradition of liberty and justice for all, we were unwilling to publicly disavow the ideal of integration that *Brown* articulated as inimical to our familial hopes and national interests. But because we were ultimately unwilling to embrace and implement the mandate of *Brown*, we reaffirmed segregation, and we justified that affirmation by indicting the institutions whose outcomes our choices produced. To justify our rejection of integration, we condemned the poor performance of the segregated urban school systems that resulted, and then used the continuing failure of those systems as evidence that all American public schooling was failing and needed rescuing by privatization.

This may seem torturous logic. But our national psyche is deeply contorted by our racial history and experience. Traditional notions of educational opportunity as the great leveler of race and class difference are so deeply embedded in our consciousness that we often deny the elementary realities that contradict those cherished beliefs. Consider that, until 1954, the nation sustained a core belief about the principle of equality of educational opportunity within a political system in which segregating students by skin color was so legally, morally, socially, and ideologically acceptable that it required a Supreme Court decision to strip the doctrine of separate-but-equal of its respectability.

When the Supreme Court ruled in *Brown* that the Constitution required integrated education, the decision reaffirmed the Jeffersonian ideal of educational equality for all Americans. Yet our education policy across the past 50 years has produced public schooling that is more segregated, everywhere outside the South, than in the decades before *Brown* was adjudicated. How is such a paradox possible? Most important, what beliefs sustain such a paradox?

SUSTAINING THE PARADOX: *POLITICS, MARKETS, AND AMERICA'S SCHOOLS*

What follows is an effort to unravel one set of beliefs that sustain this paradox through an analysis of John Chubb and Terry Moe's *Politics, Markets, and America's Schools*, published in 1990. I focus on Chubb and Moe's work because it is the most important intervention into the debate about public schools and marketplace mechanisms since Milton Friedman's initial voucher proposal in 1955, and because the contradictions at its core exemplify the paradox of betrayal and blame that I posit.

Chubb and Moe's (1990) work combines two distinct examinations of American schooling. The first develops a political analysis of how the institutional structure of American public education inevitably produces schooling failure. It offers a radical proposal for how to change that structure by replacing democratic governance with market forces. The second presents an empirical analysis purporting to demonstrate that school autonomy is the key variable that differentiates successful and unsuccessful schools. It argues that because private schools enjoy far more of that autonomy, they produce significantly higher achievement than do public schools.

The first analysis is original and challenging, and it provoked an ongoing debate about the limitations of school reforms that do not directly address, and transform, the governance of schools. The second analysis is primarily a quantitative exercise whose methods, findings, and interpretations have been justly criticized by many scholars (Lee & Bryk, 1993; Sukstorf, Wells, & Crain, 1993; Wells & Crain, 1992). My discussion concentrates on the first analysis, because it contains one of the key components of our national response to affirming integration but implementing segregation—a condemnation of all American public education that is actually based on the failures of urban schooling.

Chubb and Moe's (1990) core argument is that democratic control of public education inevitably produces bureaucracy, and bureaucracy inevitably produces ineffective schooling. Since their quantitative analysis concludes that school autonomy is "the most important prerequisite for the emergence of effective school characteristics" that produce high student achievement (p. 61), they argue that only markets can promote that necessary school-level autonomy. In their analysis, democratic control of schooling inevitably produces bureaucratic control that limits or destroys the autonomy necessary for effective schooling.

How this conflation of democracy and bureaucracy produces schooling ineffectiveness is the focus of what Chubb and Moe call their institutional analysis of American schooling. Their logic starts from the nature of the democratic process, which they describe as a game of winners and losers. Winners get to control the state's administrative apparatus, which Chubb and Moe call its public authority, and structure the rules by which it operates. Bureaucracy inevitably results from this Hobbesian struggle to control the public authority—in this case, public schooling—because the winners structure the rules to insulate their policies from change by their successors. To ensure that their policies will continue to be carried out—in this case by the many layers of U.S. school systems—the winners impose administrative controls, that is, the rules, regulations, oversight procedures, rewards, and sanctions that characterize all bureaucracies. Because these controls must be universally imposed on all schools, they are necessarily rigid, formulaic, and cumbersome. Therefore they foreclose, if not eliminate, the school-level autonomy critical to educational effectiveness. The solution is to eliminate democratic control of schooling and replace it with market control.

Chubb and Moe's analysis proved persuasive because it seemed to explain so much of what was wrong with public education. But their argument has a problem at its core. If democratic control inevitably produces bureaucracy, and bureaucracy inevitably constrains autonomy and thereby produces ineffective schooling, why are some schools, and some school systems, successful? Generations of research have demonstrated that not only schools, but entire school districts, can consistently produce good student performance. Many American suburban and small-city school systems are among the most effective not only in this country, but across the world. Even *A Nation at Risk*, the Reagan-era jeremiad that warned that educational failure threatened to drown our republic in "a rising tide of mediocrity" (National Commission on Excellence in Education, 1983, ¶ 1), admitted that "the top 9 percent of American students compared favorably with their peers in other countries" (¶ 2).

If democratic control inevitably leads to bureaucratization that inevitably produces school failure, how can school success be explained? Chubb and Moe try to address this problem by arguing that "social homogeneity" and an absence of serious problems in some schooling jurisdictions help explain school success. Chubb and Moe never specify what they mean by social homogeneity, but their examples suggest what they intend. First, they argue that social homogeneity is a political category that involves substantial agreement about education issues. As they put it, "Groups that succeed in gaining public authority for a time are not driven to formalize in order to protect their achievements from subversion by their enemies; there really are no enemies. Homogeneous polities should tend to have less bureaucratic schools" (p. 63).

Chubb and Moe (1990) then suggest that homogeneity is a demographic category, because suburban and rural schools tend to be far more homogeneous and problem-free than urban schools, and therefore far less bureaucratized. "Suburban schools are lucky. They are more likely to be blessed with relatively homogenous, problem-free environments, and, when they are, their organizations should tend to benefit in all sorts of ways as a result" (p. 65).

Thus homogeneity seems to characterize broad political agreement about the goals, policies, and practices of public education. Chubb and Moe then argue that such homogeneity is far more characteristic of suburban and rural settings than of urban areas, and that urban areas are far more heterogeneous, diverse, contentious, and problem-ridden. In their words:

> The nation's large cities are teeming with diverse, conflicting interests of political salience—class, race, ethnicity, language, religion—and their schools are plagued by problems so severe, wide-ranging, and deeply rooted in the urban socio-economic structure that the situation appears out of control and perhaps even beyond hope. Urban environments are heterogeneous and problem-filled in the extreme. (p. 64)

In 1990, when *Politics, Markets, and America's Schools* was published, approximately 32% of U.S. students went to public schools in urban metropolitan areas, 31% attended public schools in suburbs or large towns, and 37% went to school in small towns or rural areas.[1] If Chubb and Moe exempt most nonurban settings from the inevitable bureaucratization that produces schooling failure, their analysis is irrelevant to more than two thirds of the nation's schooling population. Instead, their analysis applies only to the nation's urban schools, as their indictment of "problem-infested environments" suggests.

Problem-infested environments, Chubb and Moe argue, exist primarily in urban areas and "undermine whatever homogeneity may exist" (p. 63). This country's urban areas are populated primarily by families of color, white working-class and poor families, immigrants, and other diverse groups. Because our cities are characterized by this diversity and heterogeneity, rather than by homogeneity, Chubb and Moe argue, they cannot achieve the substantial agreement about educational issues that characterizes problem-free environments.

This argument defines diversity solely as a deficit and turns heterogeneity into destructive conflict. Its rhetoric (cities teeming with diverse, conflicting interests; problem-infested environments) echoes the distaste with which the founders of American public education regarded the squalor, indiscipline, and moral chaos they perceived in the immigrant areas of American cities. It is the characteristic perception of the other that turns difference into disorder, divisiveness, and moral deterioration.

Chubb and Moe reduce the core problems of class and race stratification to an analysis of lucky victors and problem-plagued losers. (*Lucky* suggests a new category of political analysis.) The majority of American families, who live in suburban and rural settings, enjoy schools that are relatively problem free because they serve homogeneous populations. Schools that serve diverse, heterogeneous populations are problem filled and doomed to be ineffective. What purports to be an analysis of the inevitable failure of American public education turns out to be an analysis of the failure of urban public education, in other words, that one third of all our schools and school systems serving poor African American and Latino students. An analysis that cloaks itself in universal rhetoric is actually locating a far more specific failure in our nation's urban schools and blaming the ethnic and racial diversity of our nation's urban populations for this failure.

One measure of the enduring power of *Politics, Markets, and America's Schools* is that since 1990, urban schools and school systems have become the battlegrounds of efforts to replace democratic control with market forces. Proponents of vouchers and other forms of privatization have not targeted suburban or rural schools in the majority-white areas that Chubb and Moe characterize as relatively homogeneous and problem-free environments. Instead, partisans of vouchers and other forms of privatization have aimed their initiatives almost universally at urban districts and students of color, whose failing schools are the direct results of our failure to implement the equitable schooling vision of Brown.

INTEGRATION AND THE MILITARY'S SCHOOLS

A national institution that has managed significant integration since *Brown* is the nation's military. Not only are our nation's armed forces more integrated than our civilian institutions, but the on-base schooling provided to the children of our military is also highly integrated. Moreover, the substantial component of students of color in our military's schools achieve academically at higher levels than do their counterparts across the country. To investigate the characteristics of this achievement, a report to the National Educational Goals Panel by Claire Smrekar and her colleagues at Vanderbilt University (2001) analyzed the organization, governance, instructional practices, and overarching culture of the military's on-base schools. The following discussion is based on the information and analyses in their report.

Schools serving the children of our military personnel, stationed both in this country and abroad, are run by the Department of Defense Education Activity agency, or DoDEA. Some 227 DoDEA elementary and secondary schools located here and abroad serve approximately 102,000 students, a population equivalent to the Charlotte-Mecklenburg, North Carolina, school district (Young, 2003, p. 16). (Another 600,000 children of military personnel attend civilian-run U.S. public schools located near domestic military bases.) Students of color constitute approximately 40% of the enrollment in DoDEA schools, and children of enlisted personnel make up 80%. Approximately 50% of all DoDEA students are eligible for free and reduced-price lunch. Because all military personnel are subject to frequent reassignments, student mobility in DoDEA schools is quite high, at 35%.

Smrekar et al. (2001) identify high achievement for DoDEA students on the 1998 National Assessment of Educational Progress (NAEP) tests in reading and writing. Eighth-grade DoDEA students, whether attending schools in this country or abroad, scored among the highest in the nation. DoDEA African American and Latino students scored either first or second in the nation on these eighth-grade reading and writing tests. Although both groups scored lower than DoDEA white students, the gaps were significantly smaller than the corresponding gaps in U.S. schools. Moreover, results across all the DoDEA schools on the Terra Nova Reading and Writing tests display the same pattern of universal and disaggregated high student achievement.

Thus more than 200 integrated elementary and secondary schools serving more than 100,000 students produced uniformly high test score results, and particularly high scores by their students of color. This is an impressive achievement. To learn more about the nature of DoDEA schooling, Smrekar et al. (2001) analyzed the organization, instructional practice, and overarching culture of the military's on-base schools.

The organization is administered by the Department of Defense through a decentralized structure of district superintendencies that manage schools on bases throughout Europe, in the Pacific, and in this country and Cuba. This organizational structure should produce the bureaucratic ineffectiveness that Chubb and Moe (1990) characterize as the inevitable result of democratic control, since Congress, according to Smrekar et al. (2001), acts as the ultimate school board. Instead, the DoDEA's structure uses a combination of accountability instruments and a strategic-planning process that assesses and monitors the work of the decentralized districts, but also provides considerable autonomy to each military school (Smrekar et al., 2001).

Teacher quality, as reflected by educational preparation and experience, seems quite high in DoDEA schools. Teachers are paid considerably more, on average, than their counterparts in U.S. schools. Moreover, the military's schools retain their teachers far more effectively than many urban school systems. Survey results indicate that on-base teachers hold uniformly high expectations for all their students (Smrekar et al., 2001).

The 35% student mobility rate, conversely, is very high. Since the typical tour of military duty is only 3 years, the DoDEA's curriculum and instruction is organized to deal with students who will inevitably be moving to another base school. Thus all the DoDEA schools employ the same standards-driven curriculum, but there are no mandated prescriptive methods of instruction. Instead, as part of the autonomy they enjoy, DoDEA schools have created extensive, site-based professional development to adapt curriculum and instruction to the varieties of student learning styles and educational needs. A continuous-assessment system provides feedback to teachers and administrators about student progress and spurs constant instructional recalibration (Smrekar et al., 2001).

The DoDEA's Writing Assessment, for example, is a hand-scored tool that was developed from the work of the National Writing Project. (Overseas DoDEA teachers actually piloted a predecessor version of the National Writing Project.) The assessments also inform and shape the strategic-planning process that connects schools to district superintendencies, and districts to the central DoDEA administration. A series of benchmarks in key instructional areas hold districts accountable for their student outcomes (Smrekar et al., 2001).

On-base schools benefit from the military's consistent focus on education and discipline, as well as from the security and stability that flow from the provision of most basic needs. Schools and students also benefit from smaller school size, particularly in DoDEA middle and high schools. Moreover, because these smaller schools are far more integrated than their urban U.S. counterparts, students of color in on-base schools are not concentrated and isolated in large schools composed almost entirely of similar students, as they are in U.S. urban areas. The children of officers are also integrated with the children of enlisted personnel in the military's schools.

I have defined DoDEA schools as exemplars of effectiveness, particularly because their students of color produce such high achievement. Since the 1970s, effective-schools researchers have identified schools that produce successful outcomes for students of color and have defined those schools as exemplars. Other researchers have raised necessary cautions about this practice. In his important book *Class and Schools*, Richard Rothstein (2004) questions the validity of a wide range of supposed exemplars of educational success with students of color, as part of his overarching argument that the primary determinants of student schooling success are the ways in which the nation unequally distributes wealth, income, and other hallmarks of privilege.

THE VALUE OF EXEMPLARS

Rothstein's (2004) book makes an important contribution to our national educational dialogue because it focuses on how social class structures differential student outcomes such as the black/white achievement gap. In the second chapter of *Class and Schools*, Rothstein analyzes the claims of a range of supposedly successful schools and school reforms to beat the demographic odds and reduce the achievement gaps that, he argues, result from underlying social and economic inequity. Among those suspect exemplars of success are the DoDEA schools that are the subject of Smrekar et al.'s (2001) report.

Rothstein (2004) acknowledges that the DoDEA schools do succeed in reducing the achievement gap. But he argues that those successes may well result from the relative advantage of their minority students' military parents, as well as from the privileges those parents receive as military personnel, compared to the conditions endured by poor parents of color in U.S. cities.

Rothstein argues that because military families get subsidized housing, food, and health care, their basic low pay is not comparable to poverty wages in the civilian workforce. Because the armed services require at least a high school degree, education levels in the military are higher than among the urban poor. Because DoDEA schools provide high-quality early childhood and after-school services, military children are both better prepared for school and more effectively supported during schooling than are poor children in urban areas. Finally, because the military enforces schooling discipline on its soldier-parents, parent involvement in children's schooling, and parental sanctioning of misbehaving children, can be mandated by higher authorities. All these differences, Rothstein argues, preclude using the DoDEA schools as exemplars of schools that close the achievement gap between white students and students of color.

Much of Rothstein's argument is unassailable. Military poverty is different from urban poverty. Selective military recruitment does result in a somewhat more advantaged military population, compared to similar age groups in U.S. cities. Still, a 50% free and reduced-price lunch eligibility rate for DoDEA schools is quite high; the DoDEA would rank 21st out of 50 large American cities on this poverty indicator if it were a school district (Young, 2003, p. 28).

U.S. military pay through the rank of sergeant is quite low, and the child-care and preschool programs provided on military installations reach only 58% of the total need. Moreover, the programs are not free, but offered on a sliding scale, with costs shared by the DoDEA and military families. Because the military's child care is more expensive than civilian care, even the modest average monthly $300 fee can represent a significant portion of monthly salaries, which averaged less than $2,000 in 2001. Although housing is integrated and free, it is problematic on many military bases because it is old, often in poor condition, cramped, and squalid. The health care the military provides is often of very high quality, but access and availability are problematic, and long waits and delayed care are quite common.

These qualifications somewhat reduce the differences between military and civilian realities for poor families of color. Still, military life is undoubtedly more buttressed and secure, if not more privileged. But the extent of DoDEA student achievement is striking—DoDEA African American and Latino students do better on NAEP testing than almost all their domestic counterparts. Moreover, even when parents' level of education is disaggregated, students in DoDEA schools do better than children in U.S. schools whose parents have the same levels of education. It is not clear that the modest social and economic differences between military personnel and their civilian counterparts can account for such high achievement differentials.

Nevertheless, because military bases are different from urban settings, there are limits to treating the military's schooling successes as a reform model rather than as an exemplar. As Smrekar et al. (2001) demonstrate, the military creates an atmosphere in which continuous education for all personnel is emphasized, encouraged, and rewarded:

> We believe that one of the most significant factors leading to the educational success of DoDEA students is the value placed upon education and training that permeates the military community, providing the foundation for parental support and reinforcement in ways that benefit children and help promote student achievement. The culture of order, discipline, education and training in the military community creates ideal conditions for schools focused upon these principles and expectations. (p. 32)

Such an overarching military culture cannot be transplanted to civilian school districts. Nor should it. My argument, instead, is that the problem of how to create the school cultures necessary to encourage and support the high achievement of students of color is the key problem that must be solved to improve our nation's urban schooling. The DoDEA's schooling provides one example, at scale, of the solubility of that problem. DoDEA's successes indicate that school cultures can be organized to produce high levels of academic achievement by their students of color. The perspective that cultures of schooling are variable, and that their variability can support or retard students' academic achievement, is a perspective critical to producing schools that work for students of color in urban settings. What seems clear is that the DoDEA schools have produced one variant of such an effective schooling culture.

It is important to highlight the success of the military's culture of schooling with African American and Latino students for another reason. The culture of American racism, once embedded in slavery and expanded through Jim Crow, was saturated with assumptions about the intellectual inferiority of children of color. Examples of schooling success, at scale, in producing high achievement by students of color are necessary weapons against the legacy of assumptions about inferiority that still infiltrate schooling policy. It may be rankling, at the beginning of the 21st century, some 140 years after U.S. slavery was legally terminated, to still need to use examples of minority student achievement as weapons against racism. But it is unfortunately still necessary.

The success of the DoDEA schools is not a replicable model for the reform of low-performing urban schools. But it is an important example of how school cultures can be organized, at scale, to produce academic success for students of color. DoDEA schools enjoy an organizational structure that combines accountability and autonomy, and an instructional practice that uses such autonomy to develop and diversify teacher practice to meet students' learning needs. What undergirds these characteristics is a schooling culture stressing the importance of education and providing the necessary discipline and security. What results is high student achievement for all students, and particularly for students of color. In the following chapter I investigate more closely the roles of schooling cultures that support or retard the academic achievement of African American and Latino students.

The Achievement Gap and the Culture of Schooling

We have sustained so much psychic damage and so much loss of memory. Every people, in order to remain healthy and strong, has to have a grasp of its foundation story. Culture is a chrysalis—it is protective, it takes care of you. That's what cultures are for. You cannot rob a people of language, culture, mother, father, the value of their labor—all of that—without doing vast damage to those people. People need their history like they need air and food. You deprive them of that for 246 years and follow that by 100 years of de jure discrimination, and then you say with the Voting Rights Act: it's over, you just go take care of yourself! Average people do not survive that.

—Randall Robinson, "Randall Robinson Interview"

SEVERAL YEARS AGO I had an illuminating discussion with the superintendent of one of New York City's decentralized school districts during a meeting we were having. The New York University Institute for Education and Social Policy (IESP), which I directed, was supporting the efforts of an organizing group, based in a large public housing project in the superintendent's district, to improve the academic achievement of the housing project's students. The organizing group had obtained district data—attendance, test scores, and other measures—for the housing project students and had asked IESP to help analyze it. We found that although the district had acceptable overall academic outcomes, the test scores of the housing project's predominantly African American students were far below the district average. Moreover, housing project students were referred to special education, classified as learning disabled or emotionally disturbed, and assigned to full-time segregated special education classes at far higher rates than the district's white students.

It was not only the housing project students who did poorly. Across the district, African American and Latino students posted far worse test scores than those of Asian and white students. The organizing group publicized these race-based achievement gaps and started a campaign to press the district to reduce them. IESP ran training sessions for the group on key education issues and helped the group develop campaign strategies. The group's literature often included graphs, charts, and tables identified as having been prepared by IESP.

The superintendent was very direct about the purpose of our meeting. "I need your help in getting this group off my back," he explained. "I've met with them repeatedly and tried to discuss their demands. I've responded to their requests, even when it cost me a lot of staff time, given the data they wanted. But nothing I do seems to satisfy them. They constantly disrupt our school board meetings, they circulate misleading fliers in the neighborhoods, they get parents all worked up by spreading false accusations. You're clearly working with them; maybe you can get them to listen to reason."

I explained that IESP supported the group's work, but didn't direct it. Therefore we couldn't, and wouldn't, try to tell them what to do. But since the group had proposed the formation of a districtwide task force to reduce the achievement gap, I suggested that IESP could support the task force's mission.

The superintendent shook his head. "A task force is just a waste of time and energy. What your institute could do if you really wanted to be useful is to help those parents learn how to help their kids. Those kids come into our kindergartens way behind in school-readiness skills. They fall further behind as they move up through the grades. Their parents don't help them with homework, don't make them study, don't even encourage them to behave decently in class. You could do something useful if you helped the parents learn how to help their kids do better in school."

I replied that this was not what IESP did, but there were groups available to implement what the superintendent wanted. I listed several he could contact. But I kept returning to the issue of the district's achievement gap and the need to reduce it.

"Listen," the superintendent said. "I've got a big population of immigrant students in this district. A lot of their parents don't speak English. But they're totally dedicated to their kids doing well in school. They understand that you can't get anywhere in this country without a good education; they want their kids to go to college. So they're strict about homework, they're on top of the kids' learning assignments, they support the PTA, they come out to Open School Nights to meet with the teachers, and they make sure their kids don't act out. If the project parents behaved like that, we wouldn't have any achievement gap!"

THE CULTURE OF SCHOOLING

It was predictable for the superintendent to argue that the culture of the housing project's parents, rather than the culture of his district's schools, was responsible for student failure. But was he right? In the previous chapter, I argued that the high achievement by students of color in our military-base schools demonstrates that the culture of schooling can be reshaped to reduce the race-based achievement gap. But in what sense is there a culture of schooling? How can such a culture be restructured to change schooling's predictable achievement patterns? Could changing the culture of schooling in the superintendent's district really improve the academic outcomes of the housing project's students?

In this chapter I review scholarly efforts to define the culture of schooling and link those cultures to the attributes of a society's dominant class and race groupings. Then I analyze two striking accounts of African American males' coming of age, to highlight the disjunction between their development and the culture of schooling they experienced. Finally, I review the proposals of several African American scholars to restructure the culture of schooling to more effectively support the academic achievement of African American students.

The culture of schooling is what results from how a society structures, organizes, and implements its educational system. We assume such a culture of schooling when we struggle to transform the traditional curriculum canon, when we organize alternative high schools, when we develop alternative instructional methods, or when we implement alternative discipline policies. What we are trying to change, in those examples, are components of the traditional culture of schooling. In any society, the culture of schooling is the totality of the following:

- The curriculum, which structures the required content in reading, writing, mathematics, science, history, social studies, languages, arts and other electives, and even physical education
- The schooling organization through which students of differing classes, races, genders, and ethnicities are separated into different groupings for differentiated instruction and treatment
- The primary languages and the instructional methodologies through which students are taught and the underlying assumptions and beliefs about which language and which methods best suit which students
- The accountability system, which structures the standards for student achievement, the assessments that measure student achieve-

ment, the rewards allocated to students who succeed, and the
sanctions meted out to students who fail
- The discipline system, which structures the order that the schooling authority believes is required for learning and delivers the pun-
  ishments necessary to admonish the violators of that order and
  maintain the obedience of the majority of students

In societies in which education is controlled nationally, critical decisions
about particular components of the culture of schooling, such as whether
postsecondary educational opportunities should be expanded or whether
religious clothing or symbols can be worn in schools, are often decided by
parliamentary action. In this country, state policies determine many components of the culture of schooling, such as teacher certification, curriculum standards, graduation requirements, and key aspects of accountability
systems. (State-level decisions about accountability are increasingly being
made in response to federal legislation such as the No Child Left Behind Act.)
But the overall composition of our culture of schooling is an amalgam of
custom, historical, and even commercial decisions in which teacher preparation programs, unions and professional associations, textbook publishers
and test developers, and school districts and state education departments
all play a role. Ultimately, the culture of schooling reflects, and embodies,
the dominant values of each society's hegemonic class and race.

The problem, of course, is the problem that Chubb and Moe (1990)
bemoan—no society is completely homogeneous. Therefore the dominant
assumptions about the history of how the society was shaped, what constitutes acceptable language use, the justifications for social stratification,
the extent of the social safety net, the role of religion in public education,
and all the other values internalized in the culture of schooling may clash
with the values that children from minority cultures bring to school.

Much analysis, particularly in this country, has focused on how these
minority cultural values hinder children's progress in schooling. The superintendent who urged me to help the housing project parents improve
their child-rearing practices, for example, perceived his district's race-based
achievement gap as a result of deficient parental (and racial) culture. His
solution was to change that parent and family culture to better prepare
their children for schooling.

But changing parent, family, and community cultures is far more difficult than changing schooling cultures. We would make more progress
in reducing our race-based achievement gap if we focused on trying to
change the culture of schooling to better serve students of color, rather
than trying to change the cultures that have shaped those students.

THE DOMINANT CULTURE OF SCHOOLING
AND BLACK STUDENTS

The foremost explicator of how the dominant culture of a society shapes its schooling system was the French sociologist Pierre Bourdieu. Bourdieu (1970; see also Bourdieu & Passeron, 1997) defined and elaborated a concept he called "habitus," by which he meant the values, beliefs, assumptions, expectations, symbols, and rituals of the society's dominant classes. The components of habitus, or "cultural capital," as Bourdieu's American commentators came to define it, were communicated to and learned by the children of the dominant class through speech, family customs, and aesthetic experiences—at theaters, musical-recital halls, art galleries and museums, and cinemas—as well as through family rituals such as visiting, sightseeing, taking vacations, even television watching. Through these shared experiences, the families of the dominant class immersed their children in the signs, symbols, and shared milieu of their class's culture and inculcated in them the accompanying attitudes and values structuring that culture.

Bourdieu (1970) theorizes that each nation's schooling system is similarly structured by the habitus of the dominant culture. He posits that schooling culture reflects hegemonic societal culture in its ordering values, such as its time sequences and organizational structures; the views of history and language embedded in its curriculum; the assumptions about behavior, intellect, and achievement implied in its pedagogy; and the beliefs about differential student ability and career destiny built into its aspirational structure.

Bourdieu's work has generated a torrent of studies analyzing differential instruction for different classes, and identifying the hidden curriculum through which dominant societal classes impose their beliefs and values on each nation's students. In this country such studies have emphasized the disjunctions of race as well as class, since U.S. society is structured as much by racial division as by that of class, with race perhaps being the more influential factor.

Theresa Perry is one of the key explorers in this critical field. In *Young, Gifted, and Black* (2003), she analyzes the particular challenges that the dominant culture of schooling poses for black students attempting to achieve academic excellence and preserve their cultural identities. In this work, Perry develops an explicit theory of effective education for African American students, or how the dominant culture of schooling should be reorganized to promote academic success for black children. In what follows, I use Perry's analysis of the difficulties that black student face when they attempt to negotiate the dominant culture of schooling to frame two

African American narratives of coming of age in the 1960s. I then employ Perry's definitions of effective schooling for African American students to frame the work of several African American scholars who specify what teachers and schools need to do to stimulate and support high achievement for black students.

Perry (2003) argues that, because of how deeply ideologies of black intellectual inferiority have been internalized in white racial consciousness, black students face unique challenges to academic achievement:

> The dilemma of achievement for African Americans is tied to (a) their identity as members of a caste-like minority group; (b) the larger society's ideology of Black intellectual inferiority and its reproduction in the mass media and in everyday interactions; (c) their identity as members of a group whose culture is seen, by all segments of society, even other people of color, as simultaneously inferior and attractive; and (d) their identity as American citizens. The dilemmas contained in these realities . . . make the task of achievement for African Americans distinctive. (p. 79)

Perry argues that most investigations of the black-white achievement gap fail to situate the gap within this larger context of the inevitable dilemmas that institutional racism imposes on African American students. Instead, Perry claims, the causes of limited student achievement are located within black families or black culture, just as my superintendent did.

To exemplify these racially structured challenges to achievement, Perry employs Bourdieu's theories of the inculcation and use of cultural capital to demonstrate how white elites maintain their dominant societal positions. Perry argues that cultural capital (what Bourdieu, 1970, termed *habitus*) is a set of family-inherited and inculcated knowledges and practices that equip advantaged children to succeed in school. Advantaged students have families who socialize them to internalize and understand what Bourdieu defines as the "modes and use and relationship in language: relationship to and affinity for the dominant culture; styles of interaction and varying dispositions toward schooling itself" (p. 67). Consequently, advantaged students do better in school, because schools are structured to reflect the dominant classes' cultural capital and to reward students who demonstrate that they have successfully internalized it.

Two mundane incidents may clarify this argument. When I taught *The Great Gatsby* at a community college in Newark, New Jersey, one of my students pronounced *yacht* to rhyme with *hatchet*, because she had neither seen nor heard the word before. Her confusion was quickly resolved. But suppose, in her previous schooling, my student had encountered the word *yacht* on a spelling exam, a standardized test, or even an SAT session. The student would get the question wrong; is her error an indication of her limited spelling or vocabulary skills, or the result of different cultural assumptions about relevant knowledge?

Another example. In a high school class about law and American society that I observed, a teacher was making a point about a defense lawyer who violated basic legal procedure. "That's as bad as not keeping your heels together in first position," she said. Speaking with several members of the class after the lesson, I discovered that they were mystified by the ballet allusion. Was their confusion a reflection of their limited skills, or a result of the differing cultural worlds that they and the teacher inhabited?

Since many black students come to the culture of American schooling shaped by histories, beliefs, and language use that differ from those of most white students (and white teachers), Perry argues, black students are often perceived as having little familiarity with the kinds of cultural capital that schools use and value. As a result, Perry concludes, black students' intellectual and academic abilities are too often conflated with their lack of school-valued cultural capital.

From these arguments, Perry posits that an adequate theory of African American achievement must incorporate black students' experience of being perceived as intellectually inferior by their teachers because such students possess differing kinds of cultural capital. This experience creates one of the critical dilemmas that African American students must engage and resolve. Perry argues that to survive and succeed in schools, black students need to challenge schools' failure to recognize their intellectual capacity and to reward them for their academic achievement. Moreover, Perry argues, as members of a castelike group, African American students need to develop ways to endure and challenge their discriminatory treatment in schools and in the larger society. Honoring one's African American cultural heritage, language, beliefs, and practices while learning to understand and use the school's cultural capital, Perry concludes, necessitates a constant, difficult, often perilous balancing act. The two coming-of-age narratives that follow—John Edgar Wideman's *Brothers and Keepers* (1984) and Keith Gilyard's *Voices of the Self* (1991)—exemplify that perilous balancing act and demonstrate, in different ways, the life-threatening consequences of failing to maintain that critical balance.

BROTHERS AND KEEPERS: HOW SCHOOLING FAILED AN ASPIRING BLACK STAR

John Edgar Wideman's *Brothers and Keepers* (1984) is a memoir of Wideman's effort to distill the story of his younger brother's journey from ghetto youth to life imprisonment for murder and to refract his own experience through his brother's narrative. *Brothers and Keepers* evolved through a series of conversations between Wideman and his brother, Robby, after Robby was incarcerated in Pennsylvania's Western Penitentiary. From these conversations, Wideman produced successive drafts in which he tried to capture Robby's story through Robby's own voice, and Robby edited the drafts. The book alternates between Robby's narrative and Wideman's reflections, through the persona of an older brother who left Pittsburgh's Homewood ghetto on a scholarship to the University of Pennsylvania and became one of the nation's foremost writers.

As the youngest child in an achieving household, Robby is expected to follow the example of his brothers and sisters and do well in school. After several years of living in a white Pittsburgh neighborhood, Robby's parents decide to move back to the Homewood ghetto. Robby remembers his mother worrying about what might happen to him, both in the neighborhood and at school.

> She could see trouble coming. And she was right. Me and trouble hooked up. See, it was a question of being somebody. Being my own person. Like youns had sports and good grades sewed up. Wasn't nothing I could do in school or sports that youns hadn't done already. People said, Here comes another Wideman. He's gon be a good student like his brothers and sisters. . . . But something inside me said no. Didn't want to be like the rest of youns. Me, I had to be a rebel. Had to get out from under youns' good grades and do. Way back then I decided I wanted to be a star. I wanted to make it big. My way. (in Wideman, 1984, p. 85)

Robby's way becomes hanging out in the ghetto, drinking and partying. In his narrative, school is neither a terrain to excel on nor an environment for learning. His classrooms merit only an occasional mention, as a platform on which he can sing and do impersonations of politicians and entertainers. Although Robby's academic skills seem, through his narrative, quite accomplished, he gives no weight to his in-school experience. Instead, his older siblings' success in school was a target for Robby's rebellion. As he puts it:

> I'd say damn all youall. I'd think, Go on and love those square turkeys [his older siblings], but one day I'll be the one coming back with a suitcase full of money and a Cadillac. Go on and love them good grades. Robby gon do it his own way. (in Wideman, 1984, p. 89)

Robby's way becomes an increasing propensity for getting into trouble and an endless source of concern for his parents. But after a terrifying stand-off in which Robby wields a pair of scissors against his father, he is never again disciplined by his parents, and he plunges deeper into the world of alcohol, drugs, and women that the Homewood ghetto offers in the late 1960s.

Robby's climactic episode of rebellion occurs in the 11th grade in Westinghouse High School in the summer of 1968, after the assassination of Martin Luther King Jr. Robby and his group watch smoke rising from Homewood Avenue in the middle of the ghetto and then organize a student strike at Westinghouse. Robby becomes one of the key instigators. Taking the stage in the high school auditorium after the principal refuses to meet with the student council, Robby calls for Black Power and denounces the principal, the school's administration, and the teachers as zookeepers. Robby orders the few students on the stage to bring all the schools' students into the auditorium, and as they scatter he finds himself alone with the principal, the vice principal, and the school's counselor. They are livid with rage and order Robby to report to the principal's office. But as the school's full complement of students bursts into the auditorium, Robby orders the principal to leave, and the student strike begins:

> We got together a list of demands. . . . Shut the schools down all across the city, so they knew we meant business. Knew they had to listen. The whole Board of Education came to Westinghouse and we told the principal to his face he had to go. (in Wideman, 1984, p. 115)

The students negotiate with the board of education, demanding a new principal and a black history course. When the school board agrees to their demands, Robby and the other strikers are ecstatic. On Robby's initiative, a party begins, one that starts in the school and then spills out into adjoining Westinghouse Park. Robby remembers breaking into the park building to get electricity for the bands, and dancing, smoking reefer, drinking, and partying all night while the cops surrounded the park and watched, but left them alone. Robby and his friends celebrated that night as if they owned the park and the surrounding Homewood ghetto. In Robby's memory, the party becomes the high point of the strike.

> In a way the party was the end. School out pretty soon after that and nobody followed through. We come back to school in the fall and they got cops patrolling the halls and locks on every door. You couldn't get in or out the place without passing by a cop. They had our ass then. Turned the school into a prison. . . . They fixed us good. Yes, yes, yes, when we was sitting down with the Board, but when we come back to school in September everything got locks and chains on it. . . . Wasn't never our school. They made it worse instead of better. Had our chance, but then they made sure we wouldn't have no more chances. (in Wideman, 1984, pp. 116–117)

The denouement of the strike ends Robby's references to his schooling career. He remembers the summer that followed as the period when dope flooded Homewood. On the new supply of good cheap heroin, he and everyone else he knows become heavy users. Robby then makes several failed efforts to become a big-time drug dealer to reach his goal of stardom. He and his group botch an effort to buy heroin in Detroit and sell it in Homewood, and Robby becomes desperate to amass enough funding to try again. He and his friends set up a white petty criminal dealing in stolen goods for a robbery. But the setup goes awry, the fence is shot while reaching for what may have been a gun, and he subsequently dies of his wounds. Robby and his friends flee but are eventually caught and sentenced to life imprisonment for murder.

Cultures of schooling in all societies experience extreme difficulty reaching and engaging youth like Robby—angry, alienated and determined not to conform. Robby started school refusing to become a diligent student like his older siblings. He was convinced that the stage for the stardom he coveted could never be the classroom. Yet there are schools across the country that choose to work with the aspirations of students like Robby. Such schools organize curriculum and instruction around a set of cultural heroes and exemplars who are meaningful to such students and unpack the skills and capacities that those heroes need to succeed. Many of those schools also build, through their instruction, analyses of the oppressive structures of American society that close off avenues of achievement for students like Robby. They understand about their students what Robby's older brother understands about Robby:

> "Robby's chance for a normal life was as illusory as most citizens' chances to be elected to office or run a corporation. If 'normal' implies a decent job, an opportunity to receive at least minimal pay-off for years of drudgery, delayed gratification, then, for Robby and 75 percent of young black males growing up in the 1960s, 'normal' was the exception rather than the rule. Robby was smart enough to see there was no light at the end of the tunnel of hard work (if and when you could get it) and respectability. He was stubborn, aggressive and prickly enough not to allow anyone to bully him into the tunnel. He chose the bright lights winking right in front of his face, just beyond his fingertips. For him and for most of his buddies, 'normal' was poverty, drugs, street crime, Vietnam, or prison." (in Wideman, 1984, p. 220)

Robby's moment of stardom was the student strike and the resulting party. But the party ended with the school board's betrayal of the students' demands. Those demands were certainly mild, perhaps because Robby and his fellow strikers "didn't follow through" to imagine restructuring the schooling culture that denied them relevance and failed to engage them in learning or prepare them for a meaningful future. But in spite of the students' limited demands, the school board proved incapable of rethinking the culture of the schooling it provided. Instead, it chose repressive discipline.

Suppose the Pittsburgh School Board had been able to understand the depth of rage and alienation from schooling that the student strikers articulated. The board members might have considered the need for more black teachers and administrators. Or a curriculum (including one on black history) far more relevant to their students' historical and cultural experience. Or even an instructional organization based on high academic expectations for all students, including Robby. Suppose some teacher had sensed the fire of aspiration in Robby and discovered a way to engage his broad range of capacities. In his older brother's perception, Robby possesses

> "a basic impetuous honesty that made him see himself and his world with unflinching clarity. He never stopped asking questions. He never allowed answers to stop him. The worst things he did followed from the same impulse as the best." (p. 195)

In a postscript, John Edgar Wideman (1984) provides Robby's graduation speech in Western Penitentiary, when he was awarded an AS degree in engineering. Robby begins by explaining why, though he was tempted to decline, he agreed to give a graduation speech—because getting an education under conditions so extreme should be considered an honorable achievement. He hopes his attainment can set an example for other prisoners and that the authorities will see the utility, as well as the justice, in affording prisoners the education necessary to become productive citizens. Robby concludes with a summary that encapsulates his life:

> Most of us grew up in the ghettos of Pittsburgh and the surrounding area. There the emphasis was, get the most you can with the least amount of work. My education helped me to realize, though, that nothing worth having comes without hard work and concrete effort. But being shaped by the world through this "quick get-over" concept and seeing that this concept was folly, it is now time to take our lives and our world into our own hands and shape it for the better. To show our fellow citizens and our children that education is the means by which we can make a world where all men and women can truly be free to dream our own destinies and work hard and learn well and see those dreams become reality. (in Wideman, 1984, p. 241)

In the years since Robby entered Western Penitentiary, our national prison population has grown exponentially. The proportion of our imprisoned young men of color has grown even faster; one out of every four

African American males between 18 and 30 has spent time in jail or is currently incarcerated. My argument is not simply that the culture of schooling's failure to respond to students like Robby has caused this repressive waste of talent, energy, and capacity. My argument is also that restructuring traditional cultures of schooling into hospitable places to learn for students like Robby might well have spared him, and countless others, the destructive consequences of this educational failure. One of the ultimate ironies of Robby's life is that only in the culture of prison could he begin to engage the educational opportunities to actualize his rich capacities.

VOICES OF THE SELF: STREET CULTURE VERSUS SCHOOL CULTURE

Keith Gilyard's *Voices of the Self: A Study of Language Competence* (1991), published 7 years after Wideman's *Brothers and Keepers*, distills key episodes in Gilyard's upbringing as an urban African American male. His narrative focuses on his schooling and peer culture and situates within them an examination of his language development and intellectual growth.

A family move took Gilyard from the top track in first grade of his Harlem school to the bottom track in a mostly white, mostly Jewish elementary school in Jackson Heights, Queens, across the informal but powerful boundary separating that neighborhood from black Corona. Through his determination and intellectual ability, Gilyard works himself back into the top track by the beginning of second grade. His subsequent elementary school experience is an almost unbroken record of academic triumph.

> Mrs. Lehrman asked if anyone knew the difference between a house and a home. No one else in the class even attempted an answer. The perfect stage for me. I mean getting called on and supplying the correct response was exciting enough, but you knew there were other young knights who could have handled the question. To dominate the floor completely, however, was to be top royalty. And there I was, the king. "A house can be anywhere you live with walls and ceilings and floors. But it's not a home until there is love." This answer seemed to really excite the teacher. . . .
>
> I sat down as my classmates stared in amazement, probably wondering where I picked up this information. I wouldn't tell them I learned it in Sunday School. (Gilyard, 1991, pp. 46–47)

When Gilyard becomes blood brothers with a black schoolmate in a lower track, the event prefigures the conflict he is about to experience: the culture of schooling versus the demands of his peers. Gilyard tries to get his new blood brother to take school more seriously, telling him he wishes he were in Gilyard's class, the 3-1 class. His friend scoffs.

> "Fuck the 3-1 class. Y'all startin to git too much homework. Shoot, that's what's takin you so long to git back outside now. Make sure all them arithmetic problems git done right. We don't worry about all that in 3-4. I hardly ever do my homework and I still don't git in that much trouble. Shoot, you don't do yours one day and you might git a note home with your sister. Nah, I wouldn't want no one class. Don't want no class." (pp. 54–55)   '

By the end of third grade, Gilyard has positioned himself as an academically adept, intellectually nimble, successful actor within a white institution, while his identity bonds and friendships are firmly rooted within his black community. Gilyard seems to have found a way to resolve the dilemma that Theresa Perry (2003) defines as critical to successful African American academic achievement. In Perry's terms, Gilyard has learned to use his gifts and capacities to balance the multiple roles necessary for success in the predominantly white culture of schooling, while maintaining the identity ties that sustain him in his peer culture and black community.

But Gilyard's elementary school career develops as the civil rights struggles in the South explode onto northern media screens. He experiences several personal incidents of racial tension, including an outburst against him during a football game. His loyalties are directly tested when a group of black youths from Corona, including Gilyard's blood brother, disrupt a softball game in which Gilyard is playing with his Jewish friends. As the Corona boys hassle and bully the Jewish kids, Gilyard participates in the harassment, but also protects a Jewish friend by pretending to fight with him. The scene ends without serious mayhem, though several gloves and bats are stolen.

Gilyard analyzes this development as the inevitable conclusion to his efforts to maintain both school success and his bonds with his black peers. "Up to that point, due to adroit impression management, I had been able to give convincing performances before both school and street audiences. But it was inevitable that my act before one group would suffer" (p. 110). What suffers is the persona of the high-achieving student on the terrain of the school. Whaat ensues is that within his peer group, Gilyard moves into petty crime—shoplifting, raiding delivery trucks, and stealing bikes from white kids:

> I became very active, and in many ways a leader, in a cultural system in which taking from Whites was congratulated and a militant political orientation was favored over the moderate stance the school system, and the home for

that matter, would have me assume. In our group, moderation concerning issues of race relations was defined as backwardness. (p. 111)

An encounter with the criminal justice system in Gilyard's junior high school years illustrates the development of both the depth of his racial opposition and his language ability. When one of his friends is arrested and charged with assaulting a white boy, Gilyard, who wasn't present, decides to give false testimony to help get his friend off. He manages a carefully calibrated performance and holds his own against the corporation counsel's efforts to shake his story, and his false testimony contributes to the judge's dismissal of the case. He writes:

I had successfully wielded language as an instrument of power in the often-intimidating world of the legal system. This tactical success gave me greater confidence than ever in my ability to manage impressions in novel situations, using language as the primary device, and it also served as dramatic notice of a truth I was well aware of by then: inadequate language skills would not be my downfall. (p. 159)

But there is a downfall. Gilyard scores high enough on the citywide admissions test to win acceptance to one of New York City's most prestigious public high schools, and he gets good grades his first year. Then he tries heroin with some of his neighborhood friends and quickly gets hooked, just as Robby did. He returns to high school the following year obsessed with going to college, but his addiction requires money and so he turns to purse snatching, burglary, and car theft. He gets caught, is released on parole, and three days later is arrested again in another attempted robbery. This time he is sent to Riker's Island, where the city's youth jail is located. He soon gets bailed out, but faces two court cases. He returns to school and becomes a small-time heroin dealer to supply his friends and make some extra dollars, just as Robby did. Still committed to the idea of college, he scores high enough on the SATs to gain admission to and receive scholarship offers from the University of Connecticut and the University of Notre Dame. He chooses Notre Dame.

But Gilyard stays on heroin as he continues to drift through high school. He is granted youthful-offender treatment by the court in exchange for a guilty plea. Relieved of the burden of possible prison time, he manages to pass all the examinations the state requires for high school graduation. Consequently he receives credit for all his courses, even those he repeatedly cut, and is allowed to graduate. He spends the summer stealing, dealing, and shooting up. When Notre Dame revokes his admission and scholarship, Gilyard wonders whether his high school had informed the college about his drug use or his brushes with the law. He also expresses regret:

> After all those years putting in time with the White folks, they finally had the chance to leave me behind. That was bad enough, but I felt defeated among the brothers, especially in Corona, where I had been a bearer of collective hope. Sure, we all ran together, but several of them depended on me not to be an authentic loser in the end. (pp. 156–157)

A friend tells Gilyard about community college and Gilyard determines to enroll, but still cannot kick his habit. Then Gilyard reads about Jonathan Jackson, the younger brother of black militant and prison writer George Jackson who was killed in a shootout trying to free his brother. "Here was a kid younger than I who put his very life on the line because he still believed in dreams. . . . Almost as soon as I finished reading the story I knew I was out of the drug life" (p. 157).

Somehow, Jonathan Jackson's hopelessly militant act snapped Gilyard's self-destructiveness and forced him to face the future. Gilyard kicks his habit and commits himself to going to college, and the memoir ends. What we can surmise from the text is that Gilyard completed college and graduate school and transformed his doctoral dissertation into *Voices of the Self*, which won an American Book Award when it was published in 1991. Gilyard subsequently taught for many years at Medgar Evers College of the City University of New York, and he is now a professor of English at Pennsylvania State University.

In his conclusion, Gilyard examines the tension that almost ended his academic career and might have ended his life:

> I was torn between institutions, between value systems. . . . I tried to be a hip schoolboy, but it was impossible to achieve that persona. In the group I most loved, to be fully hip meant to repudiate a school system in which African American consciousness was undervalued or ignored: in spite of the many nightmares around us, I was urged to keep my mind on the Dream, to play the fortunate token, to keep my head straight down in my books and "make it." And I pumped more and more dope into my arms. It was a nearly fatal response, but an almost inevitable one. (p. 160)

The tension that Gilyard's book explores stems from his discovery of the power of racial discrimination and oppression, "the many nightmares around us," and the failure of the culture of his schooling to acknowledge those nightmare realities. The acceleration of the cycle of protest and repression in that superheated period of civil rights, black power, and antiwar activism, the same period of Robby Wideman's journey to manhood and prison, intensified the tension that Gilyard experienced between black reality and white denial. Gilyard perceived that tension as the pressure of being forced to choose between the culture of the school and his neighborhood and peer culture. For many of Gilyard's peers, as well as for Robby, the culture of schooling expected so little of them, and tracked them into such undemanding settings, that choice was nonexistent and tension was muted. Consider Gilyard's blood brother's view of the world of 3-4, where "I hardly ever do my homework and still don't git in that much trouble."

THE CULTURE OF SCHOOLING AND BLACK ACHIEVEMENT

The culture of schooling's denial of black reality produces patterns of black reaction that vary from a determination to triumph academically, as in Gilyard's example, to a rejection of, disengagement from, or rebellion against, school, as in Robby Wideman's example. Yet just as the superintendent in the vignette that opened this chapter located the causes of his housing project students' poor achievement in their parents' supposedly deficient culture, too many analysts still locate the primary causes of the achievement gap in black family structure, black child-rearing, and black youth culture. The larger failure of the culture of American schooling to recognize and respond to what Perry (2003) defines as the specific dilemmas of black students is too rarely articulated, acknowledged, and acted on.

Yet an important stream of work in this country has analyzed how the dominant culture of schooling has failed too many black students. Herbert Kohl, in *36 Children* (1998), described his development of curriculum and teaching methods that engaged, excited, and challenged his Harlem elementary school class. Shirley Brice Heath, in *Ways with Words* (1983), contrasted the languages and embedded worldviews of poor white and black southern rural families, and then examined the contrasting, and often conflicting, language and worldviews in the culture of schooling those children entered. Asa Hilliard III has focused his life's work on explicating the differences between the views of history, the assumptions about language learning, and the organization of instruction embedded in the dominant culture of schools and the history, language patterns, and learning styles embedded in African American culture. Lisa Delpit, in *Other People's Children* (1995), analyzed the ways in which the instructional methods of progressive education, an influential alternative pedagogical philosophy, often conflict with effective instruction for African American students. Gloria Ladson-Billings, in *The Dreamkeepers* (1994) and other works, identifies effective teachers of African American students and analyzes the components of their effectiveness.

These and other pioneers have contributed to an evolving analysis of the limitations of the dominant culture of schooling for black students. Moreover, their work has begun to specify how that culture should be reconstituted to produce more effective schooling. Teachers in training, practitioners in classrooms, and administrators and policy makers across the country are using their work to rethink curriculum, instruction, and school organization so that they more effectively support the academic achievement of black students.

In *Young, Gifted, and Black* (2003), Theresa Perry not only defines the necessary dilemmas that black students face when they negotiate the dominant culture of schooling. She also identifies the schooling characteristics that encourage high academic achievement in African American students:

> African-American students will achieve in school environments that have a leveling culture, a culture of achievement that extends to all its members and a strong sense of group membership, where the expectation that everyone will achieve is explicit and is regularly communicated in public and group settings. African-American students will achieve in these environments, irrespective of class background, the cultural responsiveness of the setting, or prior level of preparation. (p. 107)

In addition to pointing to a set of public schools serving black students across the country that have developed and inculcated such practices, Perry identifies schools run by the U.S. Department of Defense, which were examined in Chapter 1 in the present volume, as well as Catholic schools and historically black colleges as exemplars of cultures of schooling that consistently produce high African American achievement.

In the same work, Perry offers a definition of school cultures in which African American students experience difficulty achieving academically. In Perry's view, these are

> school communities, irrespective of class background and prior level of academic preparation, that are individualistic, committed to giving their students lots of degrees of freedom, and highly stratified and competitive and that make few attempts to build and ritualize a common, strong culture of achievement that extends to all students. (p. 107)

This characterization fits the schools that Gilyard and Robby attended. Most of the nation's schools, and particularly those attempting to serve students of color in inner cities, could be similarly described.

Perry then concludes that "institutions that are culturally responsive and that systematically affirm, draw on, and use cultural formations of

African-Americans will produce exceptional academic results from African-American students" (p. 107).

How can school cultures "affirm, draw on and use the cultural formations of African-Americans?" Examining the debate about the appropriateness of using black English in inner-city classrooms might provide an example to buttress Perry's argument. Efforts to base initial instruction on African American language use, a critical component of black culture, provoked intense controversy when such a proposal was advanced, almost a decade ago, by the Oakland, California, school board. When the board suggested including Ebonics (black English) as part of the framework through which African American students were taught, the proposal provoked a violent reaction from predominantly, though not exclusively, white critics.

Some of the response put forth by a number of opponents was based on traditional opposition to instruction advancing any form of bilingualism. Others who were against the idea derided the notion that black English constituted a language worthy of instructional use. Yet a half century of scholarly work, and particularly Labov's (1970, 1972) pioneering studies, conclusively demonstrated the formal rules, complexities, and semantic logic of black English.[1]

Teacher educators such as Lisa Delpit (1995), Gloria Ladson-Billing (1994) and others have demonstrated the effective use of black English to affirm and build on the language and culture that African American children bring to school. Their work argues for the use of black English as a platform from which to introduce and develop the use of standard English, so that black children become adept code-switchers, familiar with the languages and cultural terms of both their black and white worlds. (One of the achievements Gilyard demonstrated in *Voices of the Self* (1991) was his increasing ability to effectively code-switch between black English and standard English.)

Beyond the use of black English, Perry's argument that stimulating high achievement in African American students requires a schooling culture responsive to black cultural formation also provokes intense opposition among school practitioners and education policy makers. Gloria Ladson-Billings (1994) perceives such opposition as stemming from the inability to perceive the realities of African American culture. Ladson-Billings argues that there is

> a stubborn refusal in American education to recognize African Americans as a distinct cultural group. While it is recognized that African Americans make up a distinct racial group, the acknowledgment that this racial group has a distinct culture is still not recognized. It is presumed that African American

children are exactly like white children but just need a little extra help. Rarely investigated are the possibilities of distinct cultural characteristics (requiring some specific attention) or the detrimental impact of systemic racism. (p. 9)

Ladson-Billings's work counters this refusal to acknowledge the realities of black culture and also demonstrates how successful teachers use their understanding of those realities to stimulate and sustain high achievement in black students. In *The Dreamkeepers*, Ladson-Billings (1994) analyzes the classroom practice of five African American and three white teachers who were successful in getting African American students to achieve to their highest potential. Ladson-Billings summarizes the principles of their effective practice:

> They see their teaching as an art rather than as a technical skill. They believe that all their students can succeed rather than that failure is inevitable for some. They see themselves as part of the community and they see teaching as giving back to the community. They help students make connections between their local, national, racial, cultural and global identities. Such teachers can also be identified by the ways in which they structure their social interactions: Their relationships with students are fluid and equitable and extend beyond the classroom. They demonstrate a connectedness with all of their students and encourage that same connectedness between the students. They encourage a community of learners; they encourage their students to learn collaboratively. Finally, such teachers are identified by their notions of knowledge: They believe that knowledge is continuously recreated, recycled, and shared by teachers and students alike. They view the content of the curriculum critically and are passionate about it. Rather than expecting students to demonstrate prior knowledge and skills, they help students develop that knowledge by building bridges and scaffolding for learning. (p. 25)

Through case studies describing these eight teachers at work in their classrooms, Ladson-Billings develops specific examples that demonstrate these principles. She provides an interesting contrast in the teaching of reading. One of her teachers is a passionate believer in whole-language methods, while another is a firm supporter of the structure that basal readers and phonics provide. What Ladson-Billings shows is that, beneath the apparent opposition, both teachers share a set of classroom strategies that focus on helping tentative students, particularly boys, become intellectual leaders; that build learning communities in which student experience is legitimated and used; that employ a broad definition of literacy; and that make the classroom a site for struggle against racially embedded low expectations and for academic and cultural excellence.

Ladson-Billings believes that teachers can be trained to be effective teachers of African American students, and she concludes her book with a set of recommendations for changing teacher practice. She argues for developing teacher preparation strategies that do the following:

- Recruit candidates who want to work with African American students
- Focus their training on the critical role that culture plays in students' lives and learning[2] and immerse them in African American culture
- Help those teachers understand and critique the social sorting, economic tracking, and political disempowering role of traditional cultures of schooling
- Give teachers the experience of seeing culturally relevant teaching and devote much more time to the student teaching experience

With such preparation and training, Ladson-Billings argues that many more teachers would join her eight successful teachers of African Americans.

Several historians have argued that, in spite of the severely inadequate provision that, pre-*Brown*, kept separate education rarely if ever equal, many black teachers set a very high standard of excellence for their black students. Vanessa Siddle Walker (2001) analyzes how African American teachers in Georgia, between 1940 and 1960, developed their professionalism to provide the best possible education to their students. Siddle Walker uses archival sources and oral histories to synthesize a set of principles that define the beliefs structuring the work of African American teachers. Those principles include the following:

- Strong teacher identification with the culture and beliefs of encompassing black communities
- Active involvement with those communities, to become more effective teachers and to serve as role models for their students
- Commitment to professional ideals, involving a strong ethic of caring for students and a dedication to the teaching task that necessitates efforts to meet students' needs beyond the normal school day and the traditional classroom and school boundaries
- Adapting curriculum to meet students' needs, including making the prescribed curriculum more academically expansive and supplementing the required curriculum with information about the history, accomplishments, and dilemmas of African Americans in this country

- Effectively using a variety of supports provided by the surrounding African American community

These principles further exemplify what Perry (2003) means by the school culture, organization, and instruction of "institutions that are culturally responsive and that systematically affirm, draw on and use cultural formations of African Americans" (p. 107).

Imagine an inner-city school system that set out to implement Siddle Walker's (2001) principles. Such a school system would need to make consistent efforts to hire African American teachers from communities within the district and develop programs to encourage black parent activists and paraprofessionals to become teachers and then to support them. Such a school system would have to provide the time and support necessary for such teachers to make frequent home visits and work with the parents of their students to more effectively support their students' learning. Such a school system would have to provide extended time for teachers to work together to expand and enrich the prescribed curriculum so that it adequately reflected African American history, language, experiences, and dilemmas. Such a school system would need to develop ways to tap the varieties of supports that surrounding African American communities can provide to encourage the academic achievement of their students. If school systems serving inner-city black students could inculcate this set of principles, the nation might discover how much of the current race-based achievement gap could be meaningfully reduced.

SYNTHESIZING THE RESEARCH TO RESHAPE THE CULTURE OF SCHOOLING

What are the implications for reducing the achievement gap, from Perry's analysis of the necessary dilemmas black students face? From Wideman's (1984) memoir of his brother's perilous journey? From Gilyard's (1991) analysis of the tensions that nearly destroyed him? From Perry's (2003) definitions of successful cultures of schooling for African American students? From Ladson-Billings's (1994) investigations of successful teachers of African American students? And from Siddle Walker's (2001) analysis of the instructional beliefs of black teachers in segregated schools?

First, traditional American cultures of schooling can be restructured to produce the conditions under which black students can achieve academic excellence. Second, such reshaped cultures need to respond to the differences between black culture and dominant culture and to the dilemmas that black children confront when they enter mainstream schooling.

Third, these reshaped cultures need to inculcate high standards and demand high achievement for all students. Fourth, such reshaped cultures need to ensure that black students are taught by quality teachers. Fifth, such teachers need to establish active relationships with their students' parents and communities.

Summarizing this set of requirements makes them sound simple. Implementing them requires a systematic reshaping of traditional American cultures of schooling. One way to begin that reshaping is to rethink the system of accountability for achievement that the traditional cultures of American schooling have constructed. Because we have defined accountability in American public education primarily as an audit function that focuses almost solely on student outcomes, we habitually fail to recognize the critical ways in which schooling cultures shape how students learn—or fail to learn. In the following chapter I consider how we might rethink the nature of accountability for effective education, primarily for students of color but also for all students.

Inspection and Audit in Accountability

Educational accountability systems work—when they work—by calling forth
the energy, motivation, commitment, knowledge, and skill of the people
who work in schools and the systems that are supposed to support them.
—Richard Elmore, *The New Accountability*

I N LONDON in the 1960s, I taught at a day-release college, an institution serving young people who had left school at 15 but subsequently
decided they needed more education. I taught a liberal studies block in
the daytime, and in the evenings I taught English literature to students
preparing for their initial certification exams for career and college. One
year, the set text for the English exam, mandated by the Ministry of Education, was Shakespeare's *Twelfth Night*. I was more than 3 weeks into the
play when the college's headmaster stopped by my classroom. "You're
going to have an official visitor in your Thursday night class," he told me.
"One of Her Majesty's Inspectors is scheduled to observe your lesson."

I told him I'd never been inspected. "It's quite simple," my headmaster assured me. "The HMI will introduce himself before the class starts.
He'll be wearing a dark suit, most likely pin striped, with a blue shirt and
a dark tie. They tend to specialize in a kind of rumpled elegance." My
headmaster chuckled, perhaps because I usually taught in jeans and a
sweater. "He'll explain who he is and why he's come, then he'll take a
seat at the back of the class and observe the lesson. Some inspectors take
detailed notes, others don't. He'll pay quite close attention, but he won't
interrupt or call attention to himself. When the class is over he'll come up
and say a few encouraging words to you. That's all there is to it."

I asked if the inspector would be rating my teaching. "No, no," my
headmaster assured me. "HMI doesn't work that way. The inspector's role
is to assess the quality of teaching and learning throughout the college.

He'll present me with a detailed report of his findings, but he won't review the individual teachers he's observed. If he saw something particularly problematic, he might raise it with me, but you needn't worry. He'll enjoy your class."

That Thursday night I came to class in a jacket and tie. A tall, graying, slightly stooped man in his early sixties, in a dark gray suit, blue shirt, and maroon-striped regimental tie, introduced himself at the door. "I'm one of Her Majesty's inspectors," he said, and explained that he would be observing the class. I gave him a copy of the *Twelfth Night* edition we were using and began the lesson.

My students were all young men, mostly postal clerks, with a few London Transport bus cleaners and Covent Garden flower market porters. Most were not accomplished readers, and none had ever seen a Shakespeare play. But they had begun to pay close attention to the text and were reading their parts aloud with enthusiasm. Several had sheepishly admitted that they were beginning to enjoy the play. We would read a scene, analyze the action, unpack the metaphors, and debate the motivations of the characters. Fortuitously, a new production of *Twelfth Night* was running in the West End, London's theater district. I had seen it twice. Since my headmaster had agreed to finance a theater visit once we had finished the play, I could suggest how the staging highlighted particular plot twists and memorable speeches, hopefully whetting their anticipation of the actual production.

The 90-minute class went quickly. As the students were packing up to leave, the inspector met me at the front of the class. "Thank you for a quite interesting lesson," he said. "Very unusual, to hear Shakespearian dialogue with an American accent. Makes one think anew about some of the lines one's got used to skipping over."

I nodded, puzzled about how to respond "You do a very close reading," he said. "But for these lads," nodding toward the last few stragglers filing through the door, "you needn't focus quite so much on the underlying themes. What they need is a good grasp of the plot and the characters to get them through their O-levels [certification exams]. They're not likely to encounter Shakespeare again."

I thanked the inspector, we shook hands, and he departed. When I recounted the inspector's visit to my headmaster, I asked if I should file an official complaint about his parting comment. "Is he within his rights to ask me to lower my standards for 'these lads'"?

My headmaster nodded in amusement at me, a stance he often took. "Filing a complaint won't get you anywhere. I suggest you just chalk it off to his age; I suspect he's been at this a bit too long."

THE ENGLISH INSPECTION SYSTEM

That was my introduction to the operations of a public education account-ability system based on very different assumptions than those that obtain in this country. Across the past 150 years, the English have developed a system of inspection to hold schools accountable and to help them improve. Supposedly expert practitioners, like the inspector who observed my class, were the core of the inspectorate system. HMIs were teachers or school headmasters (and gradually, after 1950, headmistresses), selected for their deep knowledge of instruction and their capacity for astute observation and analysis. They were trained on the job, and learned their craft as apprentices, by participating in inspection visits with senior HMIs. Traditionally, teams of inspectors from the national corps of HMIs periodically inspected English schools. Local inspectors, employed by the local education authorities (LEAs), which until 1992 comprised the governance base of the English schooling system, made more frequent school visits, and followed up on the findings of the HMI inspections.

The English inspection system was originally designed to inform the national government about the condition of the nation's schools. As the inspectorate evolved, this primary purpose was complicated by the aim of informing schools about their strengths and weaknesses. Both purposes began to merge as the methodology of the inspectorate—the school visit—evolved during the 20th century. In the high period of the inspectorate's development—between 1950 and 1980—the school visit became a refined and critically reflective practice.

When an HMI team visited a school, the inspectors observed classes, interviewed the teachers, and consulted with the school's head. Inspection visits could take an entire week, during which all the school's classes were observed. At the conclusion of each visit, the chief inspector held an extended meeting with the school head in which the inspection team's key observations were discussed, and the team then reported their conclusions to the entire school staff.

Several months later, the school head would receive a report elaborating the findings and advancing a set of recommendations about how the school might improve its instruction. Because there was no tradition of administrative transparency in what was then the United Kingdom, units of government never publicly disseminated official reports. Therefore parents and community members never saw school-level performance information or were privy to analysis about how well or poorly schools were functioning. (Inspection reports were not made public until 1983, when a transformation of the inspectorate began.) Only the school's head, the governors of the school (equivalent to a board of trustees), and the LEA ever saw a copy of the inspection report.

Several assumptions about accountability were embedded in this system. First, standardized testing played no role. During the century in which the United States was developing IQ testing and then implementing standardized achievement testing, English education remained unencumbered by any form of standardized testing.

Until 1975, the only universal test English students took was a nationally administered, criterion-referenced achievement test at age 11. The 20% who passed were placed in an academically oriented school that served as the gateway to a university education for the even smaller percentage of the English age-eligible cohort that went on to higher education. (Only 15% of all age-eligible English students were enrolled in higher education in 1975.) The 80% of all English students who didn't pass the age-11 national tests were assigned to comprehensive schools that aimed to provide a more practical education for work and adult life.

The small cohort of college-bound students at the academically oriented schools took a series of national subject-specific examinations, the O-levels my day-release college students were preparing for, and the A-levels that university admission processes used as placement tests. (Both sets of exams required essays in response to set questions, or asked for demonstrations of acquired skills. Exams were scored by teams of teacher readers led by full-time professional examiners.)

However well or poorly schools prepared their students for these gatekeeping examinations, student results were never aggregated by school. Nor were schools assessed by their students' results. Not that the sparse amount of English national testing wasn't determinative. The gatekeeping examinations not only defined students' academic opportunities, but also shaped students' occupational choices, career trajectories, consequent class status, and subsequent life experience.

But in contrast to the constant rankings of schools in the United States, English schools were unranked on any measure of student achievement until the late 1980s. For most of the 20th century, an English school's reputation was developed through an often idiosyncratic process of parent, student, and teacher judgment. A school's inspection results rarely contributed to that reputation.

Accountability in this system was adherence to a code of professional practice, based on HMI judgments of what constituted high-quality teaching and learning. But these judgments were never promulgated as official standards. Just as English common law evolved through an oral tradition of accumulated court decisions, the inspectorate's values and judgments evolved through 150 years of practice.

The best available description of pre-1980 English inspection at work is Thomas A. Wilson's *Reaching for a Better Standard: English School Inspection and the Dilemma of Accountability for American Public Schools* (1996). In his book, Wilson constructs a fictitious inspection visit based on his 10 months' experience shadowing English inspectors. Wilson's reporting inspector (the head of the team) explains how he defines the work:

> "An inspector can do good when he or she has acquired a working knowledge of the school. That knowledge comes only from hard, precise, repetitive work. That is what makes good inspection. The crucial starting place is being there—observing at the school, seeing how students are or aren't learning, and coming to an understanding about what each school is all about. Each school is different. As you will see, the team spends a lot of time talking in order to come to corporate judgments about its quality. We tie our judgments closely to evidence that has been an integral part of that process. Personally, the most important and satisfying part of inspection for me has been how we finally make sense out of all the details, how we create a snapshot that has meaning for other people." (p. 112)

The inspectorate system that Wilson describes and analyzes reached its apogee in the period 1950–1980. In the early 1980s, HMI tried to restructure in response to demands for greater accountability from the government of Prime Minister Margaret Thatcher. But HMI's efforts were judged to be too limited. The Thatcher regime began a major reform of the entire education system that also transformed the inspectorate. Successive governments expanded this reform, promulgating national standards and a national curriculum, implementing a series of national assessments, and publishing school performance rankings based on assessment results. The regimes also initiated a new inspection system run by the Office for Standards in Education (OFSTED).

OFSTED's system grades schools according to specific criteria. It requires schools to develop their own evaluation prior to the inspection visit and to generate a development plan after the visit. Inspectors must use each school's national-assessment results to frame their inspection visits, and the inspection's grades become part of a broader national ranking of school performance. Finally, inspectors are no longer part of HMI, but are contracted as inspection teams that include senior teachers and LEA advisors as well as former inspectors (Wilson, 1996).

The OFSTED system set out to correct what many critics identified as the limitations of the inspection system. OFSTED incorporates national standards and the results of national assessments into inspection and schools' resulting ranking. It publishes inspection results, to provide clarity about the standards that schools are being assessed against and how well schools have measured up. What is unclear is whether the processes OFSTED implements will strengthen what the traditional inspectorate, at its best, provided—incisive analysis of school strengths and weaknesses and critical recommendations for school improvement (Wilson, 1996).

INSPECTION AND AUDIT

Michael Rustin, until 2004 professor of sociology and dean of social sciences at the University of East London, has written a challenging paper analyzing the competing purposes of English public-sector accountability systems, which he defines as inspection and audit (2003). Rustin argues that the improvement purposes at the core of inspection systems often conflict with the central purposes of audit systems—articulating common standards and measuring comparative performance.

Rustin defines the key objective of inspection systems as

> improving quality and performance, not indirectly through the incentive or punitive effects of published rankings, indicators or reports, but directly, through the learning that takes place during the interactions between the inspectors and the inspected, and in the preparations for and outcomes of inspections. (p. 10)

Although Rustin does not cite the example, the pre-1980s English inspectorate assumed such learning at the core of its practice. HMI developed a set of protocols to help schools prepare for inspection visits. Inspectors held a series of consultations with each school's head to review the inspection's focus, organization, schedule, procedures, and ground rules. Visits were designed to maximize the inspection as a learning experience to help schools improve their instructional practices.

Rustin sees this form of accountability as critical to processes of improvement in complex organizations, because change in such organizations depends on getting management and staffs to think and act differently. He writes:

> If the aim is to find out what could be improved in an organization, and to think about how to bring improvements about, a different state of mind is called for. This requires, above all, trust, between colleagues, in organizational superiors, and in external inspectors who are having to bring bad as well as good news. Trust is needed because improvement is not possible without prior acknowledgement of weakness or deficiency (without this, why

would improvement be necessary?) and no one is going to accept their own deficiencies willingly if they believe these are going to be punished when they are discovered. (2003, p. 16)

Given this need for both intra- and extraorganizational trust, Rustin advocates "a learning model for organizations," driven by core beliefs about "relationship, trust and cooperation as the preconditions for development, not only within institutions, but also in their transactions with external authorities" (p. 4). To make those transactions work effectively, he calls for accountability systems that combine the critical audit functions—the articulation of common standards and the use of appropriate assessments to measure how well those standards are being met—with inspection efforts designed to identify how effectively institutions are carrying out the necessary processes of improvement and what might aid those efforts.

The inspection efforts Rustin proposes are analogous to the HMI visits and follow-up processes of the inspection system I have described above. But there are significant gaps between Rustin's vision and the reality of how the traditional pre-1980s English school inspectorate operated. Because HMI never promulgated and disseminated standards for instructional practice, its modes of operation remained craft based and were often mystified. As my own experience suggests, the inspectorate was sometimes infected by varieties of class, race, and gender bias.

Moreover, because the inspectorate never tracked measures of school achievement, it proved difficult to assess whether inspection actually encouraged a learning relationship that resulted in subsequent school improvement. Nor were there ways to understand when that relationship was successful, or why. It was often unclear, for example, just what inspection could accomplish with schools too dysfunctional to acknowledge, let alone act on, the findings of the inspection visit. Ultimately, the inspection system could not generate any external validation of its own effectiveness. Thus the existence of substantial achievement gaps between middle- and working-class students, as well as between white students and students of color, only became widely identified in the 1980s, as examination results were disaggregated by school, race, and class and were increasingly made public.

Using Rustin's formulations, one could argue that until the national education reforms of the 1980s, English accountability efforts had privileged the functions of inspection and neglected the functions of audit. This imbalance was corrected (many argue it has been overcorrected) by the education reforms of the 1980s and 1990s, which reconstituted both the inspection process and HMI. The ongoing evolution of OFSTED may eventually realize the synthesis that Rustin's analysis calls for: an inspection system that constructively analyzes and helps to improve school-level practice, and an audit system that promulgates universal standards and assesses school-level performance against those standards.

AUDIT SYSTEMS IN AMERICAN ACCOUNTABILITY

Using Rustin's (2003) formulations of inspection and audit to examine American public education accountability systems, it is clear that U.S. practice has privileged audit over inspection. Moreover, until quite recently, U.S. accountability has emphasized only one aspect of audit systems—what Rustin identifies as the function designed to "define and measure the relative or comparative performance" over the other aspect, to articulate "common agreed standards of performance and output" (p. 4). A brief review of U.S. accountability systems may clarify this argument.

The introduction of IQ testing in the 1920s led to the development of varieties of standardized testing to place students in supposedly appropriate educational settings. I call this use of testing *placement accountability*. The use of testing results to gauge the comparative effectiveness of schools and districts began in the 1970s and has continued through the subsequent decades. This development is often defined as *performance-based accountability*.

Until the rise of the standards movement in the early 1990s, both placement- and performance-based accountability systems have been solely audit-focused. Moreover, they emphasized only one dimension of what Rustin (2003) defines as the twin functions of audit. Both placement and performance-based accountability measured student performance, but did not articulate any standards against which that performance was assessed. Instead, measurement increasingly usurped the role of standards. It became common, for example, for schooling practitioners to declare that a particular student was reading at the 60th percentile, without knowing what the 60th percentile meant, in terms of actual reading capacity, or even what reading skills the assessment was measuring.

This tyranny of numbers abstracted from context became dominant because, unlike the case in countries with national education systems, U.S. accountability until the early 1990s had not developed systems of coherent standards at either state or local levels. Instead, public education in this country, for most of the past century, has been a mélange of state and local curricula whose instructional content was driven by custom, scope, and sequence guidelines and by textbook publishers. Without a system of standards for what students should know and be able to do, testing results became, by default, the only common accountability coin.

Placement accountability, for example, assumes that students have differing abilities that require differentiated instruction and that testing can accurately identify those differences. Unfortunately in this country, this practice has been closely linked to, if not driven by, widely held racial, ethnic, class, and gender bias. The results of placement accountability have often been used to justify different expectations for different categories of students and to track students according to stereotypical assumptions of their intellectual capacity and probable social and economic destinies. The continuing use of test-based placement often makes negative contributions to teacher judgment about student capacity, as Ronald F. Ferguson argues in his chapter "Teacher Expectations and the Test Score Gap," in Jencks and Phillips's *The Black-White Test Score Gap* (1998). Ferguson writes that

> at both ends of the test score distribution, stereotypes of black intellectual inferiority are reinforced by past and present disparities in performance, and this probably causes teachers to underestimate the potential of black children more than of whites. If they expect black children to have less potential, teachers are likely to search with less conviction than they should for ways to help these children to improve, and hence miss opportunities to reduce the black-white test score gap. (p. 312)

Placement accountability systems assume a static view of the instruction that follows test-based placement. Subsequent teaching is assumed to verify placement decisions, not to transcend them. Thus placement accountability becomes both predictive and reifying; it assesses and then freezes student achievement instead of helping schools learn how to improve it.

Performance-based accountability uses standardized testing to assess the effectiveness of schools and districts and often to reward or sanction such performance. During the decades of the 1970s and 1980s, performance-based accountability was not tethered to any coherent definition of what students should know or be able to do. Instead, a mix of state and local curricular definitions, often embedded in scope and sequence guides, intersected with the efforts of textbook publishers and test developers—often units of the same corporations—to provide curricular and instructional guidance to the nation's schools.

The rise of the standards movement in the early 1990s introduced the argument that curriculum, instruction, and assessment should be anchored in a set of common standards for what students should know and be able to do. The standards movement also made a commitment, more honored in the breach, to align standards with appropriate assessments designed to measure how well students were achieving the standards.

The key criterion for such accountability systems is how closely standards, curriculum, and assessments are aligned. The critical questions become, Are the curriculum and instruction organized to teach the content and skills the standards call for? Are the practitioners sufficiently skilled to enact a pedagogy that effectively teaches the curriculum? Are the assessments designed to measure the extent to which the curriculum has been successfully taught—do students know, and are they able to demonstrate, the knowledge and skills that the standards call for?

SOME PROBLEMS OF AUDIT SYSTEMS

Although standards were developed unevenly across states and districts, many states did create some overarching standards frameworks across grade levels and major subjects. But most states and districts did not develop the assessments necessary to gauge how well the resulting standards-based curriculum and instruction were successfully embedded in students' learning experience. Because developing such assessment systems requires lengthy and costly investment, most states and districts continued to purchase and use relatively inexpensive, commercially available assessments that often were not aligned to either standards or curricula.

Performance-based accountability is an improvement over placement accountability because student results are defined as outcomes rather than as inputs. But the failure to integrate assessments with standards and curricula is a critical limitation. It severs assessment from its improvement function and reduces it to a meaningless (in instructional terms) audit response—measuring student performance but failing to contribute anything to help schools improve.

Another critical mistake of the standards movement was the jettisoning of attempts to assess whether sufficient opportunities to learn, for all students and particularly for poor students of color, accompanied the teaching and learning standards. Opportunity-to-learn standards were initially proposed as part of the national standards movement, but eventually disappeared from the movement's rhetoric and demands. But without well-developed opportunity to learn standards, students can be, and increasingly are, penalized for never having been taught what the assessments are supposedly testing. Since opportunity to learn, in this country, continues to be differentially provided by race and class, poor students of color are doubly victimized by the failure to implement opportunity-to-learn standards. First, they are denied the instruction necessary to succeed on the standardized assessments. Then they are identified as failures because they have performed poorly on those assessments.

This double failure of performance-based accountability systems has reduced those systems to routine audit functions—they identify comparative levels of school and district achievement, but offer little intervention or support to help schools improve. The underlying audit assumption of most current performance-based systems is that public identification of failure induces improvement. Presumably once they are publicly identified, poorly performing schools will be shamed into launching improvement efforts. (Or, given some states' and districts' imposition of rewards and sanctions, inadequate schools will be forced to improve through the threat of punitive actions.)

But as a host of educational researchers, reformers, and practitioners have repeatedly argued, improvement depends on capacity (Darling-Hammond, 2004; Elmore, 2002; Hilliard, 2003; Linn, 2005). If poorly performing schools had the capacity to improve their performance, they would not continue to risk being publicly identified and shamed as failures. As Richard Elmore (2002) observes:

> Low-performing schools, and the people who work in them, don't know what to do. If they did, they would be doing it already. You can't improve a school's performance, or the performance of any teacher or student in it, without increasing the investment in teachers' knowledge, pedagogical skills, and understanding of students. This work can be influenced by an external accountability system, but it cannot be done by that system. (pp. 33–34)

Because of the inability of poorly performing schools to plan their way to improvement, an effective accountability system requires inspection efforts—capacity-building and learning interventions—as well as audit functions. These capacity-building interventions are imperative in urban systems, which contain the great majority of the nation's poorly performing schools. Yet the history of state and district improvement efforts suggests too few attempts to provide such inspection—that is, capacity-building and learning interventions—to schools.

During the past 2 decades, for example, many states and districts have implemented school-based-planning programs designed to help their failing schools improve. But successful school-based planning depends on sufficient school-based capacity—the ability to analyze patterns of student achievement, understand students' skill needs, define what is necessary for improvement, and implement the policies and practices required. Schools with lackluster leadership, and with inexperienced and demoralized teachers, cannot carry out such efforts without significant district intervention and support (Ascher, Fruchter, & Ikeda, 1999, 1998; Fruchter & Siegel, 2002).

An experience some years ago brought this lesson home to me. I was serving on a New York State Education Department panel convened to review the plans of New York City schools identified as in need of significant improvement. One particular school's improvement planning had been rejected by two former panels; the plan our panel was reviewing was the school's last chance to avoid closure and reconstitution. But our panel unanimously concluded that the school's plan was grossly inadequate. We were exasperated by the plan's failure to identify the school's major deficiencies and appalled by the gap between the school's needs and the timidity of the proposed interventions.

When the school's team was ushered in for the formal review, our frustration was evident in the tone with which we began our questioning. The chair of the panel, a young math teacher, angrily interrupted us.

"I'm the most senior teacher in the whole school," she snapped. "And I've been here only 4 years! How the hell do you imagine we can write a decent plan in these conditions? We can't even figure out how to keep our kids from sneaking out of the building, or stop them from turning the lunchroom into a daily food fight. What do you expect from us?"

What we expected was a comprehensive reform plan that the school had no capacity to develop or implement. Waves of education reform based on similar expectations have swept through urban districts across the past 3 decades. But they have produced little improvement in poorly performing schools because they have ignored the critical role of local school capacity. The school-based management initiatives of the late 1980s–early 1990s, for example, were designed to encourage school-level efforts to improve instruction. Aside from the failure of those initiatives to reallocate any real power over curriculum, instruction, personnel, and budgeting to the school level, school-based management programs have provided little intervention and support to improve the capacity of the leadership and staffs of poorly performing schools (Malen, Ogawa, & Kranz, 1990).

The reform wave that heralded one-school-at-a-time change suffers from similar limitations. This reform proceeded from the supposedly research-based models of school transformation funded by the federal Obey-Porter Comprehensive School Reform Demonstration project. But successful implementation of these reform models depends on district and school capacity. Studies of efforts to implement these models demonstrate that participating schools and districts rarely had sufficient capacity to implement the reforms as designed. Worse, the national-reform sponsors did not provide support of sufficient power, depth, or complexity to respond to these capacity limitations at the local level (Bodilly, 2001; Corcoran, Hoppe, Luhm, & Supovitz, 2000).

The failure of these reform efforts generated some ambitious proposals for solutions. One popular reform of the mid-1990s called for dissolving most district authority and transferring significant power and autonomy to the school level. The rhetoric that characterized this reform stressed the necessity to free schools, particularly urban schools, from the control of ossified district bureaucracies, so that schools could actualize their own leadership capacity and teacher creativity. At core, this is Chubb and Moe's argument in *Politics, Markets, and America's Schools* (1990). But a radical intervention into schooling improvement, as described in *Reinventing Central Office: A Primer for Successful Schools*, edited by Anne Hallett (1995) for the Cross City Campaign for Urban School Reform, also advocated the devolution of many district functions to the school site. (As a *mea culpa*, I should note that I helped write that document.)

The proponents of this movement to break the constraints of district administration were focused on the successes of small, capacity-rich, often maverick urban schools. What they failed to consider (I should say, what we failed to consider) was that conferring autonomy on other urban schools with limited capacity for improvement might well cut those schools loose to founder, or sink, on their own. One of the ironies underlying the advocacy for school autonomy is that urban districts whose policies and practices had produced school failure would now be absolved from the responsibility for intervening to rectify what they had helped to create. Schools, themselves, were now to be solely responsible for their performance.

The experience of directing the evaluation of the New York Networks for School Renewal, as the Annenberg Challenge Grant project in New York City was called, convinced me that the problems of school capacity could not be solved by conferring autonomy on schools or developing school-based networks for mutual support. At one level, the New York City Annenberg project was clearly a success. The project pledged to start some 50 new small schools across 5 years, and it actually initiated more than 60. When assessed as an aggregate, the Annenberg project schools achieved higher test score gains, higher attendance, and lower drop-out rates than those of the several comparison-school samples our evaluation constructed. Moreover, the project's schools, in the aggregate, did not cream—that is, the schools did not produce their favorable outcomes by selecting and serving more advantaged students. Across the 5 years, the project's schools enrolled higher percentages of students of color, and higher percentages of poor students, than the city system as a whole, as well as all our comparison groups.

But the New York City Annenberg project's goals were more ambitious. The project design called for participating schools to form networks for mutual support, as well as for direct intervention to support struggling schools. These networks of schools were to unite to form an autonomous zone of mutual governance, which would replace traditional district forms of administration. This new "Learning Zone" would ultimately demonstrate how associations of self-governing school networks could replace the role and function of school districts.

This effort failed to consider how much school-level capacity is required to build and sustain successful schools, let alone create effective cross-school networks. Relatively few functioning networks were developed, primarily because the demanding work of running schools provided little remaining energy to devote to the tasks of building, managing, and sustaining cross-school structures. The few networks that struggled to survive never mobilized the energy to create cross-network collaboration and never managed to intervene to support struggling schools. Without the equivalent of a district structure to provide the capacity and the support to bring schools and networks together, the dream of the Learning Zone evaporated.[1]

THE CRITICAL ROLE OF DISTRICT CAPACITY

The problem of how to encourage and support local school improvement is ultimately a problem of how to improve limited district capacity. Until very recently, most districts were more focused on carrying out their management functions than on developing their capacity to improve the schools under their jurisdiction (School Communities That Work, 2002; Tyack & Cuban, 1996). Even large urban districts, with staffs of hundreds and sometimes thousands of personnel, have rarely developed consistently effective school improvement practices.

Worse, many big-city systems have developed methods of funding allocation, and procedures of student and teacher assignment, that reduce, rather than improve, school performance in some of their schools. How does this happen? Urban districts serve multiple constituencies with differing levels of economic advantage and political power. Many urban districts allocate their fiscal, teaching, and support resources to schools in response to the differential power of the constituencies those schools serve. By distributing resources to schools serving advantaged students, districts shortchange and penalize schools serving disadvantaged students and often exacerbate the resulting variations in school performance.

Many urban districts, for example, use their student-assignment power to concentrate their special education, immigrant, and second-language students in schools that, as a consequence, become dumping-ground institutions (Ascher, Fruchter, & Ikeda, 1998, 1999). Most of the students so relegated are poor students of color. Many urban districts use programs of choice, in which students choose the schools they wish to attend, to develop student-assignment policies, particularly at the secondary level, that reward advantaged schools with higher-achieving, better-behaved students. The same policies send lower-performing and more behavior-problem students to overcrowded, poorly resourced schools in poor neighborhoods. Most of the students so relegated are poor students of color. In urban districts that have retained significant percentages of white students, student-assignment patterns, particularly at the secondary school level, often produce schools with disproportionate numbers of white students at one end of the district's continuum, and similarly racially isolated schools populated almost entirely by poor students of color at the other end.

Urban districts often use their teacher-assignment policies to concentrate higher-quality teachers in more advantaged schools (Ingersoll, 2004; Lankford, Loeb, & Wycoff, 2002). Teacher union seniority policies, negotiated with school district management, aid this concentration by encouraging more senior teachers to move from less advantaged to more advantaged schools. The widespread practice of using the district-average teacher salary as the formula base for school-level funding allocation exacerbates these systematic inequities. It allows districts to pay higher teacher salaries in more advantaged schools, while paying lower salaries to less experienced teachers in schools serving poor students of color (Roza & Hawley Miles, 2002).

Teacher attrition rates at high-poverty urban schools are much higher than those at more advantaged schools. Richard Ingersoll's (2004) research indicates that because of high attrition in many urban districts, "an entire staff could change within a school in only a short number of years" (p. 2). District administrations play a key role in alleviating or worsening the school-level conditions that cause high attrition rates in high-poverty schools.

These mechanisms are examples of district practices that exacerbate inequity of resource provision, and resulting variation in performance, in urban systems. Perhaps no national reform effort has been so misused as Title I, the federally funded compensatory education effort to improve the education of poor students. Many districts, for example, traditionally skewed their provision of local funding (often called tax-levy support) to compensate schools ineligible for federal Title I funding, because of their relatively advantaged student populations. This practice was defended on the supposed equity grounds that all students, no matter what their needs, should generate the same funding.

After I was elected to my local Brooklyn Community School Board in 1983, I discovered an analysis that demonstrated that the city's community school districts distributed Title I funding with little relationship to school need (Davis, 1982). Because almost all my district's schools received Title I funding, I decided to explore the equity of our funding allocation. The district's superintendent provided the number of children in each school eligible for Title I funding, as well as the district's average Title I per pupil allocation. When I did the necessary math and compared my results to the district's allocations, the mismatches were staggering. Half the district's schools were allocated substantially more Title I funds than their eligible students should have generated; the other schools received gross underallocations. Moreover, the pattern of misallocation corresponded to the pattern of economic, social, and political advantage across the district's schools.

I distributed my findings at a subsequent working meeting of the school board, and we discussed them with the superintendent. Initially, he was nonplussed because he didn't see the purpose of the analysis. Only with difficulty did we persuade him that the each school's Title I allocation should correspond to the number of eligible children in the school. When we asked why the allocations were so far off what they should have been, the superintendent was mystified. "We've always done it that way," he answered.

Title I was originally created by a bipartisan congressional coalition committed to improving the academic performance of poor children by investing federal compensatory education funds in their schools. The evidence for the success of Title I has been vigorously disputed across most of the past half century. But both congressional partisans and opponents have been frustrated by what they perceive as the failure of states and districts to use Title I funds to reduce the nation's race-based achievement gaps. Thus, in one of the new century's striking political convergences, another bipartisan congressional coalition, spurred by a deeply conservative Republican administration, produced in 2002 what is arguably the country's first system of national educational accountability, the No Child Left Behind (NCLB) school reform legislation.

THE ORIGINS AND LOGIC OF NO CHILD LEFT BEHIND

NCLB is the latest revision of federal compensatory education aid legislation, or Title I, originally created by Congress in 1965 to allocate federal funding, through states, to school districts to help them effectively educate poor children. The core components of NCLB are actually expansions of the key regulations of the 1994 Title I reauthorization. This act tried to enhance the accelerating standards movement by imposing a set of federal requirements for standard setting, for assessments to measure achievement of those standards, and for annual incremental progress benchmarks. But because the 1994 Title I regulations had weak enforcement mechanisms, many states did little to implement them. The resulting frustration among members of both the House and the Senate helped build support for the compromise that resulted in NCLB.

Given that the Constitution, by omission, defines education as a state responsibility, how can NCLB, as a federal initiative, enforce education improvement at state and local levels? The Title I federal funding stream has never exceeded 12% of all public education expenditure and now represents only 7% of total dollars spent on public education.[2] But it is nevertheless a highly valued source of additional funding for state and local systems struggling to provide adequate resources to their public schools. NCLB requires that all state and local public education provisions, not only those programs directly funded by Title I, adhere to the new NCLB accountability regulations, for the states to continue to receive Title I funding. Although NCLB's accountability requirements pertain only to those states that choose to accept federal Title I funding, no state can afford to forego that funding in order to opt out of the accountability mechanisms that accompany it.[3] Thus a set of accountability requirements that Congress has linked to the receipt of federal compensatory funds has become, in effect, a national accountability program.

NCLB represents a new direction in U.S. accountability efforts. It requires reducing the achievement gap, not only between white students and students of color, but also between students advantaged and disadvantaged by socioeconomic factors, between mainstream students and students disadvantaged by disabilities, and between native English speakers and students for whom English is a second language. No previous national accountability effort has targeted the reduction of these achievement gaps.

How is NCLB structured to carry out such an ambitious project? First, states are required to develop assessment systems, initially in reading and math, subsequently in science, that test all students and disaggregate the testing results by race, gender, poverty level, second-language use, and disability. Next, states must develop standards for proficiency in each subject area tested and set yearly performance targets so that by 2014, all students will reach proficiency in all subjects. Schools and school districts that do not reach their annual performance targets (in NCLB terms, do not make adequate yearly progress [AYP]) in each student subcategory are subject to increasingly severe sanctions.

The penalties initially require districts to allocate funds to provide parents in failing schools with supplemental educational services, primarily tutoring, for their children. Next the penalties grant parents the right to transfer their children from schools that fail to meet their AYP targets to other more successful schools, and require districts to pay transportation costs. Ultimately, the penalties require districts to close schools that are consistently unable to meet AYP goals. States are required to identify and similarly sanction districts unable to meet their performance targets.

NCLB has other provisions, including a strengthening of parental rights and options, and a requirement that states and districts significantly increase teacher quality. The summary above is only a bare sketch of the new accountability regimen that NCLB imposes. But both the unprecedented scope of NCLB's requirements and the very problematic nature of its methodology suggest that NCLB is a triumph of audit that ignores the necessary functions of inspection.

NCLB does take a giant step toward equity of outcomes by requiring that assessment methods identify the progress of all students in a school or district, by subgroup, rather than reporting the results of aggregate student achievement. Under NCLB, inadequate performance by the groups of students American education systems have always poorly served—students of color, poor students, students whose first language is not English, and students with disabilities—can no longer be masked by aggregating their results into mainstream student achievement categories. Moreover, NCLB not only mandates disaggregated reporting of achievement results, but also requires that the measurement of adequate yearly progress be similarly disaggregated. The legislation imposes punitive sanctions not only for overall failure to achieve such progress, but also for failure to achieve it for any of the disaggregated categories of students. This is a signal achievement.

THE KEY LIMITATIONS OF NO CHILD LEFT BEHIND

But NCLB's methodology incorporates several traditional problems of American accountability systems. For example, the legislation's primary emphases are the measurement of school progress, the identification of school success or failure, and the definition of the resulting sanctions for that failure. NCLB does provide some school choice and tutoring for students in schools that fail to meet AYP targets. But the school choice options, thus far, have been very limited, and the resources allocated for supplemental services are dwarfed by the need. Moreover, both parental choice and supplemental services are individual interventions. They may help particular students, but they do not constitute inspection efforts— that is, efforts that help poorly performing schools improve.

Instead, most of NCLB's components concentrate on audit functions— the measurement of performance and the sanctioning of failure to achieve adequate performance results. Worse, NCLB's measurement processes are deeply flawed. Because Congress chose not to create a national assessment system as part of NCLB, the law gives states the responsibility to identify proficiency levels in each subject area tested, to set 12-year achievement goals, to specify annual yearly progress benchmarks, and to choose their assessment instruments. This responsibility creates strong incentives for states to rig their goals, proficiency levels, AYP benchmarks, and assessment systems.

Many states, for example, have set very low proficiency levels or established quite skewed 12-year achievement curves that consign the largest required gains in annual yearly progress to the final years of NCLB. Other states have selected assessments of such varying levels of difficulty that, for example, the proficiency level of one state's fourth-grade math test is equivalent to the proficiency level of the same state's eighth-grade reading test (Kingsbury, Olson, Cronin, Hauser, & Hauser, 2003).

The law requires that the state-level results of the National Assessment of Educational Progress (NAEP) be used as a check on the validity and reliability of state assessments. This requirement loads far too much weight on NAEP, whose validity and reliability have been challenged by scholars and researchers (Linn, 2003). Moreover, as Robert L. Linn (2005) has demonstrated, "there is only a relatively weak relationship between the performance of students in a state on NAEP and the percentage of schools that meet their AYP goals" (p. 12).

The core methodology of NCLB is the requirement that all schools demonstrate increases in absolute, rather than relative, levels of achievement across a 12-year time frame. This requirement has been universally condemned by researchers, scholars, and practitioners. James E. Ryan's (2004) analysis presents a particularly trenchant critique:

> The requirement that an increasing percentage of students in every school achieve a certain test score each year is arbitrary and unrealistic, in that it establishes achievement goals without any reference to past achievement levels or rates of achievement growth. Many schools, including some that are considered effective, will be unable to meet these achievement targets. This will create pressure to make the targets easier to meet by dumbing down the tests or making scoring systems more generous. By this process, a law intended to raise academic standards may lower them. (p. 934)

Ryan's analysis also emphasizes particular disincentives built into NCLB's measurement mechanisms:

> Disadvantaged students tend to do worse on standardized tests than do their more affluent counterparts. An accountability system that rewards and pun-

ishes schools based on absolute achievement levels will thus reward relatively affluent schools and punish relatively poor ones. Moreover, given that minorities are disproportionately poor, and that all schools are held responsible for the performance of their minority and poor students, this accountability system will tend to punish those schools that are racially and economically diverse. All of this will make racial and socioeconomic integration even more difficult to achieve than it is already, and it will provide even more incentives for good teachers to choose relatively affluent schools. These trends, in turn, make it possible that a law designed to narrow the achievement gap will help widen it. (pp. 934–935)

Ryan also points out that the pressure to reach AYP targets may lead high schools to increasingly push out students who are likely to fail the state testing that NCLB requires. Ryan argues that this increase in push-outs will raise actual drop-out rates, no matter how the push-out process is camouflaged to protect the school and the district's ranking. Many critics have also charged that the NCLB annual growth requirements, as well as the imposition of universal testing, unfairly penalize students with disabilities and English-language learners.

These problems at the core of NCLB's measurement methods continue the tradition of American audit, which privileges measures of test performance over more complex assessments of achievement designed to help schools learn how to improve. Yet schools and districts will be forced to learn how to improve, or learn to manipulate their outcomes to counterfeit improvement, to escape the punitive sanctions that NCLB imposes. Real or counterfeit, the scale of improvement necessary will prove quite costly, and predictably NCLB funding has failed to meet that cost. The law continues the federal legislative tradition of what has come to be called unfunded mandates. Many congressional representatives claim that the compromise liberals and conservatives negotiated to pass NCLB included a commitment from the administration of President George W. Bush to significantly raise Title I funding to meet the new law's stringent accountability requirements. But the Bush administration has not allocated the additional funding the law requires.

The traditional disclaimer that more funds won't make a difference will not resolve this problem. The ongoing difference among scholars about whether, and how, money matters in education is narrowing. James Coleman's (1966) Equality of Education report to Congress concluded that family background affects student achievement far more than does resource investment. The resulting policy conclusion, that money doesn't matter, once represented the consensus about resource provision in education. Eric Hanushek's series of reviews of the research on the relationship between resources and achievement (1989, 1994, 1996) helped to validate this conventional wisdom. But more recently, Hedges and several colleagues have reanalyzed Hanushek's work and have challenged his conclusions (Hedges & Greenwald, 1996; Hedges, Laine, & Greenwald, 1994). Their research demonstrates strong relationships between school spending and student achievement. Alan Krueger and Richard Card have carried out similar analyses and generated similar findings (1996). On balance, a judicious summary might be that the research now suggests that resources, appropriately invested, do make a difference.

There is also a long tradition of argument about the necessity to provide adequate opportunity to learn standards, to assess whether the preconditions for achieving the requirements of legislation such as NCLB are in place, particularly for poor students and students of color.[4] Even if research could conclusively demonstrate the limited relevance of funding to schooling outcomes, such a demonstration would not prove that the failure to provide adequate opportunity to learn has no relationship to poor student achievement. As the majority New Jersey Supreme Court opinion in *Abbott v. Burke* stated:

> If the claim is that these students simply cannot make it, the constitutional answer is, give them a chance. The Constitution does not tell them that since more money will not help, we will give them less; that because their needs cannot be fully met, they will not be met at all. It does not tell them they will get the minimum, because that is all they can benefit from. (quoted in Wilentz, 1990, p. 375)

I have some direct experience of these funding issues. I am one of the founders, and currently the vice chair, of the Campaign for Fiscal Equity (CFE). CFE successfully sued to force New York State to change its funding formulas to provide New York City public school students the state constitutional guarantee of a sound basic education (*Campaign for Fiscal Equity v. State of New York,* 2002). At the core of CFE's argument was the contention, buttressed by reams of detailed evidence, that the state's funding was not sufficient to allow New York City to provide adequate opportunities to learn to its public school students.

An example: The New York State Regents' regulations require all students to pass five state-level examinations—in English, math, biology, American history, and world history—to graduate from high school. Yet CFE's research into teacher qualifications in New York City high schools revealed major deficiencies in the teacher background and preparation necessary to effectively teach those subjects. A 1999 board of education report indicated that of the more than 10,000 uncertified teachers then working in the New York City school system, 476 taught high school biology, 52 taught high school chemistry, and 435 taught high school mathematics. Using conservative class-size estimates, CFE researchers calculated the number of students those uncertified teachers were attempting to instruct. According to those calculations:

- Almost 60,000 students were taught high school biology by uncertified teachers.
- Some 19,000 students were taught high school chemistry by uncertified teachers.
- More than 54,000 students were taught high school mathematics by uncertified teachers. (*Campaign for Fiscal Equity v. State of New York*, 2002)

Such failure to provide adequately prepared and trained teachers, particularly for students of color in urban areas, is not ordinarily factored into studies attempting to demonstrate the relationships between funding and student achievement. But it is impossible to argue that student outcomes are not affected by the quality of their teachers, and especially by the inability of their teachers to effectively impart instruction in subject areas in which students must demonstrate proficiency to graduate.

The failure to provide adequate teacher quality is one of the persistent failures of opportunity to learn imposed on students of color in urban schools. Unless opportunity-to-learn standards are included as integral components of national accountability efforts such as NCLB, it will prove impossible to assess the extent to which failure to meet outcome targets is actually failure to provide the necessary resources.

THE ULTIMATE LIMITATIONS OF NO CHILD LEFT BEHIND

When NCLB fails to significantly improve schooling outcomes across the nation's schools, and is consequently scaled back or substantially modified, it will primarily be because of its reliance on inappropriate and deeply flawed measurement methods. But ultimately, NCLB's limitations are more severe. The Center on Education Policy's (2005) report on Year 3 of the No Child Left Behind Act identifies the core problem:

> The most serious signs of trouble ahead has to do with the capacity of states and districts—in terms of both funding and staffing—to help low-performing schools and districts. The true success of No Child Left Behind depends on the day-to-day actions taken in underperforming schools and the effectiveness of the interventions provided for low-achieving students. But states and

districts told us they lacked the capacity to help all schools identified as in need of improvement. (p. 2)

The ultimate cause of NCLB's failure will be its inability to provide sufficiently powerful inspection efforts to complement its audit requirements. NCLB's designers failed to sufficiently consider the nation's most critical education problem—how to increase state and district capacity, through varieties of inspection, to improve their schools.

Because U.S. accountability efforts have so consistently privileged audit over inspection, American systems have inverted what should be the priorities of any education accountability system. Helping schools improve does require accurate assessment of educational effectiveness, but such assessment should complement school improvement efforts. Several states, particularly New York and Rhode Island, have developed inspection systems adapted from the English model. But as a nation we have imposed accountability systems that prioritize the measurement of school performance over the improvement of that performance. Because NCLB intensifies that national failure, its insistence on identifying the achievement of all U.S. students, by subgroup performance, may well be undone by its insistence on measurement rather than improvement.

The Limits of Choice

Choice is a panacea ... it has the capacity all by itself to bring about the kind of transformation that, for years, reformers have been seeking to engineer in myriad other ways.
—John Chubb and Terry Moe, *Politics, Markets, and American Schools*

FROM 1983 TO 1993, I served on the school board of one of New York City's decentralized public school subdistricts. Early in my tenure, a colleague and I convinced a majority of our board to increase the diversity of our district's program for gifted students.

The program had been initiated in the 1970s to keep children of middle-class families in our district's schools. By the early 1980s, as gentrification ratcheted up property values in several district neighborhoods, admission to our district's gifted program became highly prized. Because the district's student composition was overwhelmingly Latino and African American, the program's selection process included an accommodation for students of color, who could score below the cutoff and still be considered. But the gifted program's student population remained quite skewed. While more than 80% of the district's students were Latino and African American, only 20% of the gifted program's approximately 600 students were children of color. Thus the gifted programs formed overwhelmingly white enclaves in the three predominantly black and Latino schools in which they were housed. This disparity generated constant attacks, by African American and Latino activists, on the school board's lack of commitment to equity of access for the majority of the district's students.

The program's founders had established gifted strands in three elementary schools, and approximately 90 students were selected annually to enter the strands at the kindergarten level. Selection was based on performance on the Stanford-Binet IQ test, administered by a district psychologist. Children scoring above an admission cutoff were selected by rank score until all 90 slots were filled. All 4-year-olds living within the district's boundaries were eligible, and free busing was provided to every child selected.

My board colleagues and I set out to reduce the gifted program's racial disparity by changing the program's selection process. First, we decided that the Stanford-Binet was not an appropriate testing instrument, since the New York City Board of Education had suspended its use in the 1960s because of racial and cultural bias. We proposed that the district's administrators identify a more appropriate instrument.

Next, we decided that kindergarten entry was too young for appropriate testing and selection and proposed advancing program entry to first grade. We suggested that kindergarten teachers make the initial recommendations, hoping those teacher nominations, based on a year's observation, would provide a more grounded view of student capacity than a test score result. Because awareness of gifted programs was much more widespread in middle-class and gentrifying areas than in most of our district, applications for gifted testing were almost as skewed as the program population. We hoped that kindergarten teacher recommendations would produce a more diverse pool of applicants.

After much debate, a majority of our board agreed to move entry to the program from kindergarten to first grade, base selection on kindergarten teachers' recommendation as well as testing results, and switch from the Stanford-Binet to a more appropriate instrument. One of the board members, who served as liaison to the gifted program, asked that we hold a special public meeting to discuss our proposed changes, and the board agreed.

In retrospect, those of us committed to increasing the program's diversity were foolish for not mobilizing constituents who shared our views. We knew that the gifted program's parents were effectively networked. They shared bus lists (most students in the program were bused) and class telephone lists, and they met several times a year across all three schools. Consequently, on the night of the meeting, the district office was packed with more than 300 people, almost all white, and almost all partisans of the gifted program.[1]

The superintendent opened the meeting by presenting a brief history of the district's gifted program and the problems of its selection process and outlined the board's recommendations. Then several board members tried to speak to the changes, but constant attacks disrupted our arguments. When we opened the meeting to comments from the floor, a huge line of angry parents formed to attack our recommendations.

Parents defended the validity of the Stanford-Binet, argued that the board of education's findings of bias were politically motivated, and charged that we were caving in to "the political correctness crowd." Others objected to shifting entry to first grade because children forced to go to neighborhood kindergartens would lose an entire year of schooling (presumably because their local kindergartens were so wretched), and then be forced to switch schools and accommodate to a new setting. Still other parents argued that the gifted program's composition should not reflect the district's diversity because giftedness was not randomly distributed across the district's student population.

The superintendent and several board members tried to respond to these arguments, but we had to struggle to make our voices heard. "We fought to start this program, we fought to make it work, and we're not going to let you take it away from us!" one parent screamed. Several parents argued that trying to impose equity on a program based on selectivity would water it down. "This nation's greatness is based on excellence," one parent said. "You dilute the program by trying to make it more equal and you'll wind up destroying it." Many parents vowed to enroll their children in the gifted programs of neighboring districts if we enacted our recommendations. And this being the school board, we were threatened with a massive get-out-the-vote effort to defeat us in the next election.

I have described this meeting as far more civil than it was, because I have blocked from memory much of the invective hurled at us. Consider that these angry parents were not fighting simply to preserve their children's continued participation in the gifted program. All the program's students were guaranteed their placements throughout their elementary school career. Moreover, the program had a sibling variance to ensure that families could keep all their children in the same school.

These enraged parents were fighting to protect the program's selectivity and to ensure that its academic quality would not be threatened, because they assumed that increasing diversity would reduce the program's effectiveness. They were prepared to send their children to predominantly black and Latino schools, but they were adamant about maintaining an academically advanced and overwhelmingly white track within those schools.

That meeting was my introduction to the fierceness with which selective educational programs are pursued. Faced with this outpouring of parent anger, several board members reconsidered their support, and our majority for reforming the gifted program disappeared. Similar polarizing conflicts across 10 years of school board service taught me the intensity of the core tension in U.S. public education—balancing the schooling choices families demand for their children with the demands of equity of opportunity and outcomes for all children.[2]

CHOICE AND EFFECTIVE EDUCATION FOR BLACK STUDENTS

Dr. Howard Fuller has been in the eye of this storm for half a century. As a Black Panther, a youth worker, an organizer and strategist for integration movements in Milwaukee, and the leader of a citywide struggle for an all-black community-controlled school district, Fuller has been a committed leader in the fight for black children's schooling equity. Currently professor of education and director of the Institute for the Transformation of Learning at Marquette University in Milwaukee, Fuller was director of the Milwaukee County Department of Health and Human Services in the 1980s, and superintendent of Milwaukee Public Schools from 1991 to 1995. He is the president of Black Advocates for Educational Opportunities, a national advocacy group for the expansion of choice for black children. Since leaving the Milwaukee superintendency in 1995, he has been a leading national voice for choice programs for inner-city black students.

Fuller presents a challenging case for choice, as the liberation of black students from the tyranny of school districts that consistently impose inferior education on them. Fuller defines choice as the expansion of the educational opportunities available to African American children, through public programs that provide charter schools, vouchers for children to attend private schools, tax credits, and scholarship opportunities. His paper, *The Continuing Struggle of African Americans for the Power to Make Real Educational Choices* (2000), is a good demonstration of how he builds his case.

In that paper, Fuller presents the national choice debate as a conflict about power. He argues that low-income African American parents want the same power to choose appropriate schools for their children that more advantaged families have exercised for generations. Fuller frames his argument for choice by presenting a history of the Milwaukee school system's consistent refusal to provide black children an effective education. (Fuller's doctoral dissertation analyzed how the Milwaukee school system frustrated the efforts of the city's black community to integrate the city's schools.) Fuller also uses the findings of national studies to demonstrate that the failure to effectively educate black children is national in scope, historically consistent, and the result of a massive failure of political will.

The evidence for Fuller's argument is incontrovertible. As a nation, we have failed to effectively educate most African American children, and we have sustained that failure through deliberate acts of educational policy. The problem, for me, is in Fuller's solution. Will the power to choose alter this systemic denial of effective education to black children?

Part of the problem involves how Fuller conceives changing existing power dynamics. In his view, the power African Americans seek has to be granted to them by the majority white society. As he writes:

> The disparity in African American and white opinion (about how well schools are serving their children) arises, in part, because more African Americans are disenfranchised when it comes to the power to choose the best educational options for their children. The unacceptable conditions described [in the studies Fuller cites] will not change unless African Americans seek and get the power to make educational choices, a power taken for granted by most white parents. Without that power, African Americans are disarmed when it comes to holding educators accountable for providing an effective education to their children. (p. 4)

But if the power to choose appropriate education for one's children flows from economic, social, political, and racial advantage, how will that power devolve to African American families? Fuller might well respond that the decision of the U.S. Supreme Court—which ruled that a publicly funded voucher program established for poor children in Cleveland was constitutional—has granted African American families the power to choose, for he was writing before that 2003 decision (Fuller, 2000, p. 2). Now that the Supreme Court has decided the issue, choice programs—based on vouchers, charters, and scholarships—may well proliferate in urban school districts across the country. But will those programs benefit low-income African American students and their parents? The newly granted power of black families to choose will be pitted against the power that more advantaged families have successfully wielded for decades. Will the power to choose transform the landscape of existing privilege so that the newly available choices improve black children's educational opportunities?

Fuller argues that choice embedded in market-driven systems will create more meaningful schooling options for black children. But market-driven systems in this country have never been characterized by distributional equity. Black and Latino inner-city neighborhoods have never been well served by supermarkets, pharmacies, banks, hospitals, or cinemas, in spite of the power to choose of consumers in those neighborhoods. Whenever equity components have been imposed to make market-driven systems less economically stratified, they have been introduced by government and maintained by government regulation.

Fuller knows these realities intimately; he has struggled against them for decades. Yet the core of his argument is that conferring the power to choose on low-income African American families will allow them to transcend the inequities of resource distribution that disparities in economic, social, political and racial power impose. It is as if Fuller believes that the power to choose will trump the existing power that decades, if not centuries, of congealed privilege has conferred on more advantaged families.

SOME RESULTS OF CHOICE SYSTEMS

Research into public school system choice has demonstrated some benefits for lower-income and minority family choosers. Mark Schneider, Paul
Teske, and Melissa Marschall (2000) carried out a comprehensive study
of choice programs in Manhattan's District 4 and in Montclair, New Jersey, and compared them to comparable districts without choice. Their
conclusion is instructive:

> It is clear from our data that public school choice can enhance school per-
> formance and that choice can lead many parents (including low-income
> parents) to change their behavior in a positive manner. However, and this is
> where we cannot endorse choice as a "silver bullet" to cure the ills of urban
> education, while these effects are usually (but not always) statistically sig-
> nificant in our analyses, they also tend to be relatively modest in size. . . . it
> is hard for us to characterize public school choice as a cure-all for the many
> problems of urban education. But since true panaceas are rare, and espe-
> cially so in urban districts characterized by poverty and neighborhood blight,
> we should not lose sight of the many positive gains from public school choice.
> (pp. 266–267)

This measured assessment of choice's positive results is far from the
totalist claims that Fuller (2000) makes for choice. Fuller might well respond that Schneider et al. (2000) studied broad and comprehensive choice
programs within public systems, whereas Fuller argues for vouchers or
other market mechanisms that would enable black students to attend private schools. Moreover, Fuller advocates for programs specifically targeted
to low-income African American families. But once choice programs become available as marketplace options, will targeted programs for low-
income families survive against families wielding economic, political, and
social power to shape choice programs to maximize their own children's
opportunities?

In *The Market Approach to Education*, an analysis of the early years of
the Milwaukee Parental Choice Program (MPCP), John Witte (2000)
traces the evolution of the city's much-debated voucher program. Witte
describes a process in which business interests, conservative foundations,
and the Catholic Archdiocese of Milwaukee teamed with key leaders of
the Milwaukee African American community, including Fuller, to create a voucher program (the MPCP) targeted to poor African American
and Latino students. Witte argues that these same constituencies and
interests then transformed the MPCP into a more universal voucher program accessible to more advantaged white students. If choice becomes

widely available, how will low-income African American families counteract the ability of such powerful forces to use choice to further their own interests?

THE CONTEXT OF CHOICE IN URBAN SETTINGS

In his conclusion to *The Underclass Debate*, Michael Katz (1993) demonstrates how processes of migration, marginalization, exclusion, and isolation have created and reinforced the poverty of inner-city families of color. Katz's analysis describes how the development of American racism differentiated European immigrant experience from the migration experience of African Americans. Katz shows how subsequent processes of deindustrialization and globalization marginalized urban African American and Latino workers and their families. His analysis demonstrates how a variety of national and local policies, from housing and urban renewal to highway subsidy and taxation, favored white and advantaged families, privileged suburban expansion, excluded families of color from varieties of supports, and exacerbated their isolation in deteriorating inner-city enclaves (pp. 440–477). The plight of New Orleans's poor black residents, which the aftermath of Hurricane Katrina in August 2005 so dramatically demonstrated, illustrates Katz's argument.

The interlocking nature of these macroprocesses has produced inner-city schooling that consistently fails to educate the children of low-income African American, Latino, and other inner-city families (Self & Sugrue, 2002; Rury & Mirel, 1997).[3] But the processes that have isolated and marginalized poor black inner-city resident are not simply local manifestations of hegemonic white power. The actions of the federal government also played a major role. As Self and Sugrue (2002) argue, "In its haste to underwrite the expansion of an inclusive white middle class and to unfetter capital from wartime constraints, the federal government helped to exclude the urban poor, increasingly large numbers of whom were black and Latino, from the cycles of occupational mobility and personal and familial capital accumulation that define life chances in American society" (pp. 25–26).

Fuller (2000) pits the power to choose against these countervailing forces that continue to constrict the schooling opportunities of inner-city children of color. But choice seems a limited weapon against such systemic institutional racism. The major political, social, and economic gains for low-income African American and Latino families in this country have been won through periods of mobilization, organizing, and struggle for broad collective goals. The successes of the civil rights movement resulted from decades of community-wide efforts to overturn unjust laws and policies and to achieve enforcement of laws and policies guaranteeing equality of treatment and opportunity. While there is an important debate about the limits of what the civil rights movement achieved (Bell, 1987; Reed, 1999), few scholars dispute that its efforts have transformed the realities of life for American citizens of color.

The demand for choice seems unlikely to play a major role in building community mobilizations to oppose the denial of educational opportunity to low-income families of color. Certainly choice programs can change the educational experience of particular families. But choice seems unlikely to disrupt or transform the interlocking structures of power and racism that have imposed inferior education on children of color for decades.

One possible argument is that the struggle to achieve choice for black students is the contemporary continuation of the civil rights movement. Several choice advocates have taken that position. Former secretary of education William Bennett declared that school choice was "the next great civil rights arena. It has to do with equality of education and opportunity. I think choice gives poor children the kind of opportunities that only middle-class and wealthy children have now" (quoted in Holt, 2000, p. 89). Mikel Kwaku-Osei Holt (2000), editor and associate publisher of the *Milwaukee Community Journal,* Wisconsin's largest-circulation African American newspaper, took a similar stance in *Not Yet "Free at Last,"* writing that

> the crusade for school choice was a fundamental civil rights issue—one that redefined the Black agenda, refocusing our attention from failed assimilation and school board antipathy to Black self-determination and community building. (p. 100)

Jack Dougherty's *More Than One Struggle* (2004) could also be adduced as evidence that the fight for choice is another chapter in the efforts of Milwaukee's African Americans to achieve effective schooling for their children. *More Than One Struggle* documents a half century's battles to achieve equity of access and outcomes for Milwaukee's black students. Dougherty describes a series of campaigns to induce the Milwaukee system to hire black teachers, to force the system to desegregate, to stop the system from closing effective black schools, and to form a black community-controlled subdistrict within a city that was "named the most segregated major metropolitan area in the United States in 1981" (p. 187). It could be argued that the fight for choice for Milwaukee's black students is the next step in this seemingly unending civil rights struggle.

But efforts to implement choice programs across the country have never developed the broad community mobilizations that characterized the civil rights movement. Instead, as in Milwaukee, elite white interests, allied with church constituencies, have mounted choice efforts and tried to enlist black community leadership to support them. Where community mobilizations have engaged in choice efforts, they have organized to oppose, limit, and defeat choice and privatization efforts. In New York City, for example, an intensive campaign by black and Latino parents and community groups defeated the efforts of the Edison Schools Corporation to take over five poorly performing public schools by a four-to-one voting margin. In Philadelphia, a coalition of students, community groups, and the teachers union forced a significant scaling down of the school system's plan to give Edison the management of some 60 failing schools (Saltman, 2005). Thus far, constituency mobilizations organized to limit or defeat choice have been more effective than mobilizations to implement or extend choice.[4]

Ultimately, the argument that choice represents a continuation of the civil rights movement reduces the scope of that epic effort. The civil rights movement forced the nation's judicial and legislative systems to extend, to citizens of color, the rights guaranteed by the nation's constitution. The movement fought to abolish racist, unconstitutional laws at federal, state, and local levels. It used the affirmative power of the law and the courts to transform illegal, discriminatory, and racist practices. The movement also organized the power of moral witness through demonstrations that attacked the evils of segregation, racism, and discrimination. It mobilized public will to spur the ameliorative activity of a broad spectrum of American citizens. Improving the education of students of color was, and still is, a critical component of those efforts.

But choice is, at best, only a tactic, and as Schneider et al. (2000) indicate, a limited one, in the ongoing struggle to achieve effective education. The overarching goal of the civil rights movement was the collective empowerment and enfranchisement of a people who were historically enslaved and subsequently discriminated against, rather than the conferring of the power to choose on individual families. The choice argument substitutes the expansion of individual options for the transformation of societal institutions. Choice subordinates efforts to achieve collective justice to the extension of individual and familial capacity.

CHOICE AND EXIT, VOICE, AND LOYALTY

Late in his elegant treatment of the key issues of exit, voice, and loyalty in political organizations, nation-states, and private firms, Albert Hirschman (1970) argues that one cannot really exit from a public good such as education. As he writes, "A private citizen can 'get out' from public education by sending his children to private school, but at the same time he cannot get out, in the sense that his and his children's life will be affected by the quality of public education" (p. 102).

To argue that there is no effective exit from public education is difficult to sustain when urban school systems so severely damage the lives of children of color. Fuller has expended decades of effort to transform Milwaukee's schools, and he knows firsthand the depth, intensity, and obdurateness of white opposition. He argues for choice as a way to challenge and disrupt resistant school systems and to force change by introducing marketplace mechanisms. Against my fear that such marketplace mechanisms will not provide quality education to black students, but will instead further advantage already privileged white students, Fuller might well respond that the risk is worth taking. What calculus can effectively assess that decision?

My pessimism about what market mechanisms produce leads me to expect dispiriting results for black children's education. My analysis of the relationship between economic and political power and the distribution of private and public goods indicates that only sustained and effective grassroots organizing can produce more equity of education for children of color. The problem is the stranglehold that American institutional racism has imposed on the education of students of color. The solution is the organization of sufficient countervailing power to disrupt that stranglehold, rather than to provide choices for individual families. Conferring choice on individual families fails to mobilize the power necessary to confront the systemic institutional racism that structures U.S. public education. (I present some examples of organizing efforts to build that necessary power in Chapter 6.)

But Fuller has been at the center of grassroots struggles against racism in education for decades. He may well have concluded that, given the economic and political power entrenched against providing equity of outcomes for students of color, accommodation with sectors of that power can create critical new space for advancing quality education for black children. Choice, in his view, may well represent that accommodation and opportunity.

My experience differs in fundamental ways from Fuller's. My children suffered through many of the limitations of urban public schools, especially during their middle school years. But they are white, not black, and relatively privileged, and they were not forced to attend segregated public schools in Milwaukee. My experience in struggles for more equitable education suggests that choice will not produce the transformations Fuller hopes for. But my anger at the continuing damage that recalcitrant school systems inflict on children of color sometimes leads me to wish that Fuller's gamble on marketplace solutions could succeed. Those of us committed to making public schools work for all children have a special responsibility to the generations of students whose futures have been constricted during the struggle to make schooling more equitable and more effective. We need to work at least as hard to improve poorly performing urban systems as we do to oppose solutions, such as market-driven choice, that we believe will further reduce the quality of education those systems provide. My tenure on the Brooklyn school board taught me both how necessary and how difficult it is to sustain this balance.

While I was on the school board, a group of parents became so dissatisfied with their neighborhood school that they petitioned us to allow them to organize a new, districtwide school of choice. Because they objected so strongly to how their existing school tracked students for instruction, they envisioned a nontracked elementary school with a student composition that would be one third white, one third black, and one third Latino. They designed a lottery system to ensure that the selection process would produce the student mix they wanted.

The school board was hesitant to approve the new choice school, because we weren't comfortable rejecting the principle of student assignment to neighborhood schools. We knew that many parents, usually those who were more advantaged, tried to evade their assigned local schools by creating false addresses to get their children into the district's more desirable schools. We knew that many principals colluded with these efforts. We knew that our district's attempts to enforce geographic assignment were often unsuccessful. Still, we were uneasy about the implications of a formal district policy endorsing choice. Moreover, a few of us were wary that any choice program, however well intentioned and committed to equity of access, would inevitably be manipulated to serve advantaged white parents and their children.

Our district principal's association took a strong stand against the new school. The principals argued that choice would siphon off the most able students and the most active parents, thereby reducing academic diversity in and draining critical parent support from the neighborhood schools. Because the principals were convinced that, no matter how students were selected, choice schools would inevitably become elite schools, they argued that creating a choice school would exacerbate the race and class tensions already roiling the district. Finally, they argued that the instructional innovations the choice parents were advocating could be implemented by existing neighborhood schools.

The parents supporting the choice program countered these arguments. They were articulate, tireless, persuasive, numerous, and racially and ethnically diverse. Aside from the principal's association, the opposition to choice was small and scattered. But one of the district's active Latina PTA officers objected strenuously and persistently. "I worry about where the resources to create this new school will come from," she told the school board. "We've been struggling every year with the damage the budget cuts are doing to our schools. I'm afraid that creating the new school will take precious resources away from all our other schools. We can't afford to do that to our kids."

After several months of debate, the school board approved the new choice school. The school quickly proved so effective that the district started several other schools of choice and eventually created a districtwide choice program at the middle school level. Some years later I met the Latina activist at a choice school graduation ceremony. Her son was among the graduates.

"I haven't forgotten how much I was against the new school," she told me. "But when I saw how successful the school was, I knew I didn't have any choice. I had to do what was best for my son."

Thus public school choice came to my district, through the organizing efforts of a group of diverse and determined parents. I was a reluctant convert. But I have become convinced that the resulting districtwide choice program increased opportunities to learn for all the district's students and improved their educational outcomes. I now think that broad public school choice programs, carefully structured and implemented to ensure equity of access and outcomes, can contribute to improving academic achievement, particularly for students of color in urban settings. I also believe that such programs must be zealously monitored and evaluated. The persistent pressure from advantaged parents and complicit districts to transform choice programs into clusters of privilege and inequality requires constant resistance.

THE CHOICE EXPERIMENT IN NEW YORK CITY'S DISTRICT 4

Modern proposals for choice in public education began in 1955, when economist Milton Friedman argued that monopoly conditions in U.S. public education reduced schooling effectiveness and proposed universal vouchers as a market solution to ensure quality education. Supporters of Friedman's argument usually cite, as evidence for the success of choice, the experiment initiated in the early 1970s in District 4, a school district encompassing Manhattan's East Harlem neighborhood. What follows is an examination of that choice experiment and its results, primarily through an analysis of the story of the District 4 choice program, written by one of the program's architects.

District 4 is just north of the city's wealthy East Side and was a very poor neighborhood, predominantly Puerto Rican and African American.[5] The district began as one of the 32 decentralized subdistricts established by a state legislative compromise to end a wrenching conflict between the city's teacher union and African American and Latino advocates of community control of public education. The district's new young superintendent, Anthony Alvarado, faced a difficult task in raising student achievement, because District 4 ranked near the bottom of the city's 32 districts on reading and math test score results. Alvarado decided to create a series of new small schools, which quickly evolved into a districtwide choice program that Chubb and Moe (1990) defined as "the most radical—and most promising—exercise in public sector choice" in the nation (p. 212). Seymour Fliegel, the first head of District 4's Office of Alternative Schools, describes that evolution in *Miracle in East Harlem: The Fight for Choice in Public Education* (Fliegel with MacGuire, 1993).

Miracle in East Harlem defines the mission of District 4's pioneering schools as recuperative. The new schools set out to rescue children who were unresponsive to or badly treated by traditional schooling—which is why the first choice schools were called alternative schools—and to redirect them toward successful academic achievement. As Fliegel explains:

> In the early days in District Four, we didn't talk much about choice, we talked about creating good schools. The first item on our agenda was to create schools that were at once stronger and more flexible, schools that were alive and inspiring, schools that better fit the needs of the district's children. To do this we harnessed the energy of teachers—committed teachers with dreams of new types of schools, who did not balk at running their own alternative schools despite almost endless problems with the district's and the central board's bureaucracy. And the more schools we started, the more we noticed that the parents and the kids were all making choices and that this act of choosing was crucial to the success of the school. So we started to talk about taking it (choice) even further. (p. 97)

The first District 4 alternative schools were created by teachers committed to new forms of schooling, rather than by parent demand for choices that provided exit from their neighborhood schools. But demand soon followed supply. Fliegel (1993) explains the transition from an alternative-school movement to a districtwide choice system as a necessary response to the successes of the new schools. "As the population of the schools swelled so did the competition to get in, and this posed new problems. We had to devise a system that allocated kids to schools in an equitable manner" (p. 98).

That system became a districtwide or universal program of choice at the middle school level. Students and their parents were asked to choose any three of the district's middle schools, as the culmination of a selection process that included districtwide dissemination of information packets, school visits, and districtwide school fairs. According to Fliegel, the district managed to grant about 60% of the students their first choice. Some choice was also developed at the elementary school level, although the district maintained a majority of neighborhood-zoned elementary schools. Annually, only slightly more than 20% of the district's elementary school students participated in the choice program.

In the district's universal middle school choice program, students and parents chose schools, but schools ultimately chose their students. Because the test score data Fliegel provides are not disaggregated by school, we don't know what the range of performance was across the district's choice schools and whether that range was influenced by the different capacities of the choice schools to select their students.[6]

Fliegel's narrative does demonstrate that as the number of new schools increased, and as choice became universal at the middle school level, parent commitment to those new schools mushroomed. At key points during the development of schools of choice, district and citywide opposition forced Fliegel and his allies to mobilize parents to defend the choice schools. The response was always gratifying. Parents showed their support by volunteering in the schools, by assisting teachers in the classrooms, and by demonstrating through their presence at meetings and rallies how much the schools meant to them.

Through these early experiments, District 4 developed a system of choice schools that made some contribution to a significant level of districtwide school improvement. Student achievement, as measured by test scores, rose steadily across the district. Reading test scores accelerated fourfold. In 1974, according to the data Fliegel cites, less than 16% of the district's students were reading at grade level. By 1988, almost 63% were. In 1974, the district ranked near the bottom of the 32 decentralized districts in reading achievement. By 1988 the district's ranking had risen to either 15th or 17th in the city, based on some variance in the data. Fliegel also cites significant increases in the number of District 4 students enrolled in good city high schools, as well as in exclusive private schools through scholarship programs. The creation of schools of choice and the development of a universal middle school choice program contributed to a substantial increase in student achievement.

But although District 4's efforts steadily increased student achievement for more than a decade from 1974 to 1988, student performance never reached the citywide average in either reading or math. Moreover, District 4's increased performance occurred within a consistent, though less steep, citywide rise in achievement. As District 4's scores rose from less than 16% of its students reading at or above grade level in 1974 to almost 63% in 1988, the citywide average rose from almost 34% reading at or above grade level in 1974 to 65% in 1988 (Fliegel, 1993).

Moreover, the test score gains in District 4 were achieved across elementary as well as middle schools. Since there were many more students and much less choice at the elementary level, and the data Fliegel presents is not disaggregated, we cannot tell how much of the district's gains reflected increases in elementary students' performance.[7] Therefore we cannot determine how much the choice program contributed to the district's student achievement increases. What we do know is that in 1982, only 15% of the district's elementary and middle school students— 1,800 in 17 schools—were in choice programs. So in the middle years of the district's test score rise, some 85% of the district's students contributing to that rise were not in the district's choice programs (Feller, 1982).

When District 4's achievement is viewed across a longer time span, its test score performance actually rises and then falls, though the decline seems less steep than the rise. According to Fliegel's (1993) data, achievement results in 1988 mark the highpoint of the district's success. By 1993, when Fliegel's book was published, the district's reading scores had been falling for several years, and the gap between the district's scores and the citywide average was increasing. The percentage of district students accepted into the city's most selective high schools was falling, and the district ranked 23rd out of 32 districts in reading.

To demonstrate District 4's gains, Fliegel reports the district's annual position in test score performance among the 32 decentralized districts. In *Choosing Schools: Consumer Choice and the Quality of American Schools*, Schneider et al. (2000) carefully examine the issue of District 4's test score performance across time. Their analysis shows a very sharp increase in District 4's reading and math scores, compared to the citywide average, from 1977 to 1983, and then a more gradual decline from 1983 through 1996. In reading, for example, the district moves from a performance level of 60% of the citywide average in 1975 to almost the citywide average in 1983. Reading performance then falls steadily throughout the 1980s and early 1990s, and levels off at about 85% of the citywide average from 1991 to 1996. The district's math performance shows a similar, though somewhat flatter, trajectory.

Schneider et al. (2000) argue that this pattern represents a success for the choice programs in District 4. But as I pointed out previously, the district's performance cannot be attributed solely to its choice programs. The analysis in *Choosing Schools* uses all District 4's schools to construct the average trajectory of the district's performance across time. That average performance includes the scores of all the district's elementary schools, though only 21% of the district's elementary school population was part of the choice program. Thus Schneider et al. include the test scores of a majority of the district's students who were not participating in the choice program in their demonstration of the success of choice. This aggregate usage masks the actual extent of improvement in test score performance that choice in District 4 contributed.

Schneider et al. (2000) argue that the effectiveness of the choice programs at the elementary level undoubtedly influenced, and helped to improve, the performance of the majority nonchoice elementary schools. But they introduce no evidence to buttress this assumption. Moreover, as both Fliegel's (1993) data and their own evidence indicate, average test score performance improved across the city, as well as in District 4, throughout the 1980s and 1990s. It is certainly possible that citywide interventions and improvements, particularly at the elementary school level, influenced the pattern of test score rise in the majority of District 4's elementary schools not involved in the choice program.

What is clear is that District 4 experienced a rapid and sharp increase in test scores during the period in which choice programs were introduced. What is also clear is that the district subsequently experienced a test score decline. In Schneider et al.'s (2000) analysis, that drop in performance was not as steep as the increase. But as they demonstrate, not only did citywide test score performance improve across the same period, but "many lower-scoring districts started to score closer to the city average in tests administered in the 1980s" (p. 193). This rise in the scores of previously poorly performing districts raised the floor of performance citywide, and clustered districts closer to the citywide average. Thus District 4's 1996 test score performance, at 85% of the citywide average, ranked it in the bottom half of citywide district performance. By 2005, District 4's scores placed it in the bottom third of the city's districts. The miracle Fliegel (1993) narrated and celebrated had been substantially reversed, and the success of the choice programs that Schneider et al. demonstrated had substantially diminished.

THE CAUSES OF DISTRICT 4'S RISE AND FALL

No reform is infinitely sustainable. District 4's improvement in student achievement lasted longer than explanations based on varieties of Hawthorne effects would have predicted. But if school choice is to have the capacity to improve student achievement that its proponents claim, it is important to understand what affects the sustainability of choice programs. In a now-famous passage from *Politics, Markets, and America's Schools,*

Chubb and Moe (1990) argue "that choice is a panacea . . . it has the capacity all by itself to bring about the kind of transformation that, for years, reformers have been seeking to engineer in myriad other ways" (p. 217).[8]

Given such claims, it is important to explore why one of the nation's most celebrated choice programs, located in a very poor urban district and serving an overwhelming majority of students of color, could not sustain its increases in student performance. What can explain the vulnerability of this choice effort and help us understand the cycle of sharp increase and then decrease in test score performance?

Some evidence in Fliegel's (1993) account suggests that the success of District 4's choice program, and its adaptation by other districts across the city, may have contributed to its eventual decline. Fliegel describes a districtwide adaptation of choice in neighboring District 3, New York's Upper West Side, as well as substantial choice initiatives in other districts. In 1987, Anthony Alvarado, who had initiated the choice experiment in District 4, became superintendent of central Manhattan's District 2 and launched a districtwide program to create schools of choice. By 1993, District 2 had developed choice programs at both the elementary and middle school levels. The development of all these new choice programs may well have affected District 4's efforts to sustain its choice program's success.

One key issue that makes choice vulnerable in low-income districts is the recruitment of creative teachers to lead the choice schools. If such teachers are in scarce supply, the expansion of choice programs throughout the city may well result in the more creative teachers being recruited to the city's more advantaged districts. Fliegel's (1993) narrative indicates that District 4's efforts to recruit teacher directors and teaching staffs for the new schools transcended the district's boundaries. In his account, the growing reputation of District 4's schools of choice attracted creative teachers from across the city. The teacher networks that Alvarado, Fliegel, and the other school pioneers had access to also helped them recruit new teachers.[9]

Thus the creation and support of District 4's choice schools was dependent on a citywide supply of effective teachers. The development of new choice schools and programs in other districts may have so intensified the competition for teachers that District 4 could not successfully recruit the creative teachers they needed.[10] Alvarado suggests a similar explanation in an interview with Richard Elmore in which he reflects on the District 4 experience from the perspective of his subsequent success in Manhattan's District 2:

> "My strategy there [in District 4] was to make it possible for gifted and energetic people to create schools that represented their best ideas about teaching

and learning and let parents choose schools that best matched their children's interest. We generated a lot of interest and a lot of good programs. But the main flaw with that strategy was that it never reached every teacher in every classroom; it focused on those who showed energy and commitment to change. So, after a while, improvement slowed down as we ran out of energetic and committed people." (in Elmore & Burney, 1999, p. 267)

High-poverty districts such as District 4 will be vulnerable to the loss of such energetic and committed teachers unless citywide policies ensure equity of teacher-quality distribution across districts. In New York City, teacher recruitment to choice schools was unconstrained by such policies. This pattern of implementing choice as a relatively unregulated mechanism has, in other settings, produced similarly inequitable results (Fiske & Ladd, 2000, 2001; Henig, 1998, 1999; Wells, 1993).

Did the same dynamic affect the flow of high-performing students into, and then out of, District 4's choice schools? The number of students from out of district enrolled in District 4 was not insignificant. Fliegel (1993) estimates that in 1993, "almost every District 4 school has fewer than 8 percent of its entering class from outside the district boundaries" (p. 102). A districtwide rate of 8% out-of-district students would yield about 1,100 students per year, given the district's average population of 14,000 students across those years.

Later in his narrative, Fliegel (1993) asserts that "the district's reputation is so widespread across the city that over a thousand students stream into East Harlem every morning to take advantage of its outstanding schools" (p. 191). Eleven hundred out-of-district students, if the majority of them were high performing, may well have helped to increase the district's test score performance. Several critics have argued that a citywide skimming process attracted high performing students to District 4 and elevated the district's test scores. When those students' home districts developed choice programs, critics argue, those students or their equivalents may well have returned to their local choice schools, and their departure may have depressed District 4's test score performance.

Schneider et al. (2000) attempt to demonstrate the limitations of this explanation. When they control for student demographics, the results of their analysis show "that a higher proportion of higher socio-economic status students, possibly coming into the district from other locations, does not explain District Four's improved performance" (pp. 192–193). Though higher socioeconomic-status students may not correlate exactly with higher-scoring students, the overlap is close enough to accept Schneider et al.'s conclusion that the flow into, and subsequently out of, District 4's choice schools did not significantly elevate and then depress the district's test scores.

The critical explanation for the decline in District 4's achievement probably involves a reduction in district support for choice schools. Fliegel (1993) stresses the persistent opposition to choice, both from within District 4 and across the city system. Fliegel's narrative describes his office's efforts to keep district and citywide bureaucracies from interfering with the choice schools. From Fliegel's account, the following functions of his office and the district's support system for choice schools emerge quite clearly. That support system did the following:

- Recruited creative school leaders as teacher directors and helped them define their new schools' vision and mission
- Helped these teacher directors recruit their teaching staffs
- Helped the teacher directors and staffs recruit parents and students
- Helped identify and resolve school organizational problems and conflicts
- Secured necessary resources
- Protected the schools from destructive interventions by both district and central bureaucracies
- Disseminated information about the program's schools of choice to parents and the District 4 community through a variety of formats and venues
- Designed, implemented, and constantly improved the selection process of the districtwide choice program
- Publicized and celebrated the program's success and collected and disseminated data that corroborated that success

These functions are the reciprocal of the autonomy that choice partisans cite as the primary condition for school success. Fliegel's narrative demonstrates that schools of choice need such support from an external entity (in District 4's case, its Office of Alternative Schools) to survive and flourish. If that support is not forthcoming or begins to diminish, the academic performance of choice schools may well decrease.

Fliegel's (1993) narrative suggests that the district's commitment to maintaining these necessary support systems faltered, because of corrosive opposition from within the district as well as from the citywide central administration. Alvarado left the district's superintendency in 1983 for a short reign as chancellor of the citywide school system. Fliegel himself left the district in 1988 to become a superintendent in District 28 in Queens. (With several colleagues, he subsequently established a citywide center for the creation and support of schools of choice.) Although the district's Office of Alternative Schools continued under new leadership, Fliegel's narrative indicates that the district faced a host of internal and external challenges that reduced its ability to continue to support its choice schools.

THE ROLE OF DISTRICT SUPPORT

Thus district support may be at least as critical as autonomy to sustaining schools of choice. First advanced by Chubb and Moe (1990), the argument that the extent of autonomy from bureaucratic control is the key variable that distinguishes effective from ineffective schools has become a choice mantra. But what the District 4 experience demonstrates, in its arc of test score rise and fall, is that the extent of autonomy is hardly the sole determinant of school success. District 4's performance trajectory across the 3 decades between 1974 and 2005 indicates that schools of choice need extensive district supports as much as, if not more than, they need significant autonomy. For much of the period of District 4's success, the district's Office of Alternative Schools provided the operational and instructional supports necessary to sustain the choice schools. The ultimate irony of the District 4 miracle is that, according to Fliegel's (1993) account, the central bureaucracy and much of the district's bureaucracy were kept off the choice schools' backs by another part of the district's bureaucracy, the Office of Alternative Schools.

All schools, not only schools of choice, need varieties of support to become successful schools and sustain their effectiveness over time. The most obvious forms of support are operational. To focus on their primary mission of providing instruction that produces successful student learning, schools need to be relieved of the burdens of personnel, fiscal, maintenance, and other ancillary functions.[11] Most district administrations have developed effective procedures for implementing those functions so that schools can concentrate on their academic missions. But schools also need external help and support to fulfill their academic missions successfully. Here districts, particularly urban districts, have been far less successful. The persistent failure of urban districts to improve their poorly performing schools has generated several major reform movements across the past half century, including the alternative-schools movement of the 1960s and 1970s, and the charter school movement that began in the early 1990s.

I helped found, and then codirected, an alternative high school in Newark, New Jersey, in the early 1970s. As part of the initial wave of alternative schools licensed by state education agencies as private schools, our school was unconstrained by state or local regulation. The only courses the state required us to offer were American history and physical education.

Our school was free to all our students. We were able to charge no tuition because the U.S. Justice Department's Law Enforcement Assistance Administration (LEAA) and New Jersey's Title 20 program supported the school, along with a set of foundation grants. Since the LEAA funded us as an experiment in juvenile delinquency prevention, our only selection criteria were that all incoming students had to have left high school without graduating and had to have at least one arrest and conviction on their juvenile records. (Our LEAA funding required us to provide the Newark police department with our students' Social Security numbers so that they, and we, could track recidivism. We reduced recidivism to about 6%, a quite remarkable achievement.)

We offered a core curriculum of reading, writing, math, social studies, and (occasionally) science, with popular electives in art, music, pottery, carpentry, and photography. (Our school building was a former venetian blind factory renovated to provide classrooms; an art studio; a darkroom; a carpentry shop; and eventually, a full kitchen for school meals.) We also developed an extensive counseling component and a work-study internship cycle. Because the school was tuition free, attendance was essentially voluntary. Our only sanction was to terminate a student's enrollment, but students terminated themselves more frequently.

Although most of our students had dropped out of Newark high schools, a sizable percentage had left high schools in the surrounding suburbs. Because at least 10% of our students were illiterate, and had camouflaged their inability to read through a series of often-brilliant strategies, we turned one of our classrooms into a lab that taught students basic literacy. Thus our skills levels ranged from beginning readers to students who could read at high school levels, and everything in between.

Once we met the challenge of establishing the school, some of our students began considering college as a possible next step. So we started tutoring programs to prepare our students for the SATs and instituted a college advising program to help them choose and get accepted into local (and occasionally national) colleges.

Our initial SAT results were quite dispiriting. While our students from suburban or Catholic school backgrounds did reasonably well, most students from Newark schools did terribly. We saw little evidence that our 2 or 3 years of alternative high school experience had made a significant difference to these outcomes. However, as we learned how to make our SAT tutoring more effective, and as students considering college took more seriously the need for adequate academic preparation, our SAT results improved. We also developed relationships with area colleges so that we could persuade college admissions officers that our students' strengths were not reflected in their SAT scores.

Our students' subsequent college persistence and college graduation rates were similarly mixed, and the mix predictably reflected our students' backgrounds and previous educational experiences. Economic hardship also intervened. Many of our graduates who enrolled in college were forced into start-stop patterns by the necessities of work. But many of our graduates had not developed the reading and writing skills, the study habits, and the analytic disciplines necessary to succeed in college. I came to believe that what our school contributed to improving our students' abilities was not enough to counteract the effects of their inadequate prior education. I am convinced that we transformed the experience of schooling for almost all our students, and improved the academic capacity of most of them. I am not convinced that we improved those capacities sufficiently to change their predictable futures.

The alternative-schools movement of the 1960s and 1970s that my high school was part of has many similarities to the current charter school movement. Like charter schools, most alternative schools were state licensed and unencumbered by district governance or bureaucracy. The trade-off at the core of charter school philosophy—autonomy for effectiveness—was what we fervently believed at the Newark alternative high school. We were convinced that, freed from bureaucratic constraints, we could provide a more effective environment for learning than the traditional high schools our students had exited. We were certain that our efforts would produce higher student achievement.

Like charter schools, most alternative schools were initiated by groups of teachers and parents (and sometimes students, at the high school level) committed to specific ideas about more effective school organization, curricula, and pedagogy. These alternative schools struggled, as charter schools currently do, with issues of adequate space and funding, and with how to manage operations issues such as insurance, payroll, taxes, accounting, and audits. Most important, these alternative schools struggled, as charter schools do, with issues of curriculum development, teacher recruitment and support, and how to create and sustain an instructional program that effectively met students' academic needs. (Unlike charter schools, the alternative-schools movement did not emphasize the critical role of student choice, because the movement defined itself as providing alternatives for students poorly served by traditional schools and systems.)

Our alternative high school taught me how difficult it is for a few years of nontraditional schooling to overcome the background factors and previously poor schooling that depress students' sense of academic competence and intellectual capacity. Our school was independent of constraining regulation and bureaucratic impediment, but it was also independent of institutional support for operations functions and for curricular, instructional, and professional development. The scale of transformation we sought required far more resources, expertise, and institutional supports than we could muster.

CHARTER SCHOOLS AND THE PROBLEM OF INSTITUTIONAL SUPPORT

In 1999 the New York University Institute for Education and Social Policy (IESP) launched a multiyear study to analyze how New York City charter schools develop the institutional supports critical to sustaining their existence and effectiveness. This research effort, culminating in *Going Charter in New York City* (Ascher, Jacobowitz, McBride, & Wamba, 2000; Ascher, Echazareta, Jacobowitz, McBride, Troy, & Wamba, 2001; Ascher, Echazareta, Jacobowitz, McBride, & Troy, 2003; Ascher, Cole, Echazareta, Jacobowitz, & McBride, 2004), focused on two categories of schools: charter schools just starting up and alternative public schools converting to charter status.

As the charter schools developed, our research began to focus on the institutional partners most of the schools came to depend on for support. (These partners became known as educational management organizations, or EMOs.) Of the approximately 10 schools whose charter experience we tracked across 4 years (a few schools folded during that period), most developed partnerships with either nonprofit or for-profit EMOs. (A few charter schools in our study did not negotiate any institutional affiliation.)

IESP published four reports as part of a continuing investigation into "going charter" in New York City. A cumulative narrative emerges from these reports that illuminates the experience of charter schools operating in the absence of districts and the supports districts traditionally provide. Although the charter schools in our study were initiated by educators with different school visions, all the founders were committed to creating schools with theme-based curricula, student-focused instructional organization, a reflective teaching culture and collaborative parent-school relationships. (The conversion schools had already developed education practices that fulfilled their distinctive missions. An important component of the conversion schools' charter motivation was to ensure the autonomy necessary to maintain their unique effectiveness.)

Each of the start-up charters encountered unexpected and draining operational pressures that constrained their attention to instructional issues. Problems of adequate space, funding, personnel, hiring, payroll, record keeping, insurance, and a host of other issues demanded constant attention. Since New York State's fiscal policy funded charters at less than the per-student allocation to public schools, and since capital costs were not included in the allocation, most charter schools struggled with fiscal demands associated with finding and securing adequate space. The conversion schools struggled with a different set of problems—how to extricate themselves from the administrative, fiscal, and personnel arrangements that had previously bound them to the New York City Board of Education. (Ironically, though perhaps predictably, this extrication process proved so difficult that two of the conversion schools in our study eventually reaffiliated with the city system.)

Most of the charter schools in our study attempted to solve this initial set of operational problems by developing a range of EMOs as institutional partners. As the study explains,

> The institutional partners took on many of the managerial and business tasks seldom asked of traditional schools. "We're the school's infrastructure," said a member of an institutional partner. Another representative spoke of the need for "systems" which an institutional partner is able to provide. "New schools have to create policies, procedures, risk management strategies, human resources, payroll, and so forth." The institutional partners often provided all these functions. This representative recalled meeting the principal of a charter school without a partner. "He was doing payroll on the train ride up to Albany. He is a remarkable guy and was way overtaxed." (Ascher et al., 2001, p. 17)

Those charter schools that remained independent were sustained by consistent support from their initiating organizations, a foundation, and an education reform organization. The conversion schools had already developed their own support organizations. A conversion-school administrator stressed the importance of such support:

> Frankly, I don't see how a new school can do it without a support system [that offers the benefits of experience]. Most people who start charter schools are well-meaning, but they go through unnecessary difficulties, because they don't know what it takes to run a school. (Ascher et al., 2001, p. 11)

Many of the EMOs took on much of the fund-raising that was a consistent pressure on almost all the schools. As Ascher (2003) and her colleagues indicate:

> Nonprofit organizations focused largely on private gifts and foundation grants, while for-profit institutions raised private capital from their investors. Both nonprofit and for-profit partners employed full-time development staff, who wrote federal and state grant proposals, coordinated letter writ-

ing campaigns, sponsored benefit dinners, and gave school tours for corporate, foundation, and individual funders. (Ascher et al., 2003, p. 4)

As institutional partnerships with EMOs assumed some of the major operational demands, the charter schools in our study began to address the teaching and learning issues critical to school effectiveness. Personnel issues became a key function. Because most teaching staffs were new and inexperienced, burnout was a common phenomenon and teacher attrition was an annual problem. (This was not true in the conversion schools because their staffs were mostly composed of seasoned and experienced veterans.) Again, because of staff inexperience, curriculum development required outside expertise, as did the professional development necessary to raise the level of staffs' teaching skills. Helping teachers effectively respond to the wide range of student learning styles also required outside expertise, as did developing the curriculum and instructional capacity necessary to respond to students with disabilities and to English-language learners. Most charters increased both their reliance on and collaboration with their institutional partners to meet these teaching and learning needs.

The charter schools in our study experienced significant tension between their internal notions of accountability and New York State's accountability requirements. The state law requires all charter schools to administer the state's standardized assessments and authorizes the chartering agencies to use the testing results to assess whether the charters have met the achievement targets their applications specified. Several charter schools argued that the performance assessments they had developed were more responsive to their curriculum and instruction than the testing the state imposed. Other schools argued that the state's testing threatened to reduce the content and richness of their curricula and create destructive pressures of teaching to the test. But the schools' EMOs often stressed the necessity to align both curriculum and instruction with the state's testing, to ensure that assessment outcomes would meet the demands of the recertification process.

The new charter schools were committed to building professional teaching cultures based on reflective practice. Teachers in each school often had clear ideas about how to build such reflective cultures. But the pressure of daily tasks, combined with the teaching staffs' high levels of inexperience, forced the schools to turn to their institutional partners to help them construct and sustain the teaching cultures that would anchor their schools' effectiveness.

Because both the new charters and the conversions were required by state legislation to apply for recertification after 5 years of operation, all the schools in our study were concerned about preparing for the recertification process. Ensuring that test score results were adequate was only one of the constant preoccupations. Most of the charter schools increasingly relied on their institutional partners to help them develop evaluations that would contribute to preparing for recertification.

Finally, these burgeoning relationships between charter schools and their institutional partners required formalization. The New York State law authorizing charters requires all charter schools to appoint boards of directors. Moreover, EMOs cannot be granted charters; each charter school must create its own independent board; it can then contract with an EMO (which also has its own board). Therefore, although several of the charters in our study started out with informal arrangements with institutional partners, the need to formalize those relationships increased as the charter schools' reliance on those external partnerships intensified. Thus most charter schools' boards developed detailed contractual arrangements with their institutional partners that formalized their relationships.

This chapter opened with a quotation from Chubb and Moe (1990) declaring that choice is a panacea that can transform U.S. education. My argument throughout this chapter has been that choice is not a panacea, and that all the varied forms of public school choice must be carefully regulated to ensure both equity of access and equity of outcomes. Moreover, both the experience of District 4's choice program and IESP's research on charter schools emphasize the critical role of supports external to the school.

The downward trend in District 4's student achievement curve, for example, seems to have been caused by the deterioration of district support for the choice schools. Across the years of our research, the charter schools we studied created a complex series of institutional relationships to develop the supports that school districts have traditionally provided. My argument is that all schools based on principles of choice—charter schools, voucher-created schools, and all other schools independent of traditional school districts—need to develop the operational and instructional supports that districts have traditionally provided. Autonomy is clearly insufficient for choice school survival; institutional supports are critical.

But if schools of choice must reinvent or replicate the institutional supports that school districts should provide, why not concentrate reform on improving how districts carry out their essential core functions? That is the subject of the following chapter.

The District's Role in Systemic Reform

One of the major struggles in American education is the relationship between districts and schools.
　　—Anthony Alvarado, "Investing in Teachers to Improve Learning"

DURING THE LATE 1970s I directed an alternative bachelor's degree program for public-sector workers and community activists at a Jesuit college in Jersey City, New Jersey. Because many of our students worked for the Jersey City public school system or had children in the city's schools, our program periodically analyzed aspects of the school system's effectiveness. Working with an enterprising reporter, we produced data for several newspaper stories about the school system's poor test school performance and documented particular instances of systemic instructional failure.

An example: The Jersey City school district was receiving significant funding from the New Jersey Department of Education to provide bilingual education programs for Spanish-speaking students. Working with a local Latino action group, we discovered that the district was not providing any of the state-funded bilingual classes. When the local newspaper ran the story about the nonexistent bilingual program, state education department officials asked us for more information.

The Latino action group mobilized a large contingent of parents whose children should have been in bilingual classes, and we all traveled to Trenton to present our findings. After months of investigation, the state education department ordered the school system to implement a bilingual program. We had demanded that the school system provide enrichment programs with the funding it had essentially stolen from the Spanish-dominant students. But the state limited its requirements to providing the missing programs. (The Jersey City school district was subsequently taken over by the state for fiscal mismanagement and educational ineffectiveness.)

In the early 1980s, I was part of an effort, organized by a New Jersey education advocacy group, to develop courses for parents on how to improve their local schools. One of my colleagues had previously been hired by a northern New Jersey district to develop an alternative high school for the district's dropouts, much like the high school I had codirected in Newark. My colleague spent most of a spring developing the high school, and then recruited students throughout the following summer. The school opened in September with some 60 students. The school's official enrollment figures, the basis for the district's reimbursement by the state, were collected at the end of October. On November 1st, the district administration closed the school and fired my colleague and the other teachers. I was so appalled that I told my colleague I doubted even the most corrupt of New York City's decentralized districts would perpetrate such an outrage. He laughed at me. "You clearly don't know what New Jersey urban districts are capable of," he told me. "Maybe you don't know New York City districts that well either."

Some years later, the *New York Times* ran a story about a corruption scandal in a Brooklyn community school district. For many years, the *Times* revealed, the administration of this district had funneled Title I funds to the rabbi of a girl's Orthodox Jewish school, or yeshiva. The rabbi had used the funds to run the totally private religious academy. Neither the school nor the students who attended it were eligible for those Title I funds, which were meant to supplement the education of poor students. But presumably because the district's superintendent had decided that the school was a worthy effort, district administrators had illegally diverted millions of dollars from the district's Title I–eligible students for the yeshiva's use. My New Jersey colleague called me when the story surfaced. "I'm not sure any district in New Jersey could manage anything that corrupt," he laughed. I told him a story I'd subsequently remembered about that neighboring district.

That same superintendent had built a wall in one of his district's elementary schools serving predominantly poor Latino students. The wall was designed to separate those students, particularly the boys, from the girls of Orthodox Jewish families who attended after-school tutoring and enrichment activities at the school. A local Latino organizing group mobilized sufficient community outrage to force the superintendent to tear down the wall. The superintendent subsequently received an educator-of-the-year award from the city's Orthodox Jewish teachers' association.

Many reform advocates and veteran education observers can produce similar anecdotes of urban school district practice that victimized poor students of color. Too many urban superintendents and school boards apparently assumed that their responsibilities didn't include effectively educating other people's children. Worse, they also assumed that they could use the resources that the city, the state, and the federal government had allocated for the education of poor students of color for their own purposes.

Understanding why the leadership of urban school districts condoned such corruption requires more research into the dynamics of racism and city education leadership than U.S. scholarship has thus far managed. An exception mentioned in the previous chapter is Jack Dougherty's *More Than One Struggle* (2004). Dougherty's study documents 60 years of African American efforts to improve the quality of education that Milwaukee's public schools provided to its black students. Dougherty chronicles the school district's resistance not only to integration, but also to providing equity of schooling outcomes for black students. *More Than One Struggle* also demonstrates the depth of support for the district's discriminatory policies from the city's dominant white political, social, and economic elites. But since the book's purpose is not to probe the components of Milwaukee's racism, but to narrate the struggles against it, it does not examine why the city's hegemonic white forces fought so consistently to deny black students an effective education.

Many urban school systems that practiced such race-based corruption were located in cities in which white-dominated political machines had established considerable electoral power. The leadership of these political machines often perceived their school systems as serving other people's children, because so many of the machine's constituents sent their own children to parochial schools. Thus urban school systems dominated by machine control often became repositories for patronage and corruption.

Yet when control of those political machines shifted, patterns of school system corruption too often did not change. As transformations in urban political power have followed transitions in urban populations across the past half century, black and Latino school district leadership has often continued, and occasionally exacerbated, the patterns of district corruption and ineffectiveness their predecessors had introduced.

REFORM EFFORTS AND URBAN DISTRICTS

As urban districts solidified their reputations as sites of discrimination and corruption and most important, as ineffective agents at improving the education of poor students of color, many education reformers began to doubt the efficacy of district-level improvement. The waves of reform efforts across the past quarter century, especially those that developed after the publication of *A Nation at Risk* in 1983, questioned urban districts as appropriate sites for reform, because of repeated demonstrations of district incapacity for improvement.

Several prominent national reform efforts in the late 1980s and early 1990s began to bypass urban districts and initiate programs focused on individual schools. The Coalition of Essential Schools, Success for All, the New American Schools, and Accelerated Schools, for example, developed programs to help individual schools improve their instructional core, professional culture, school climate, and achievement outcomes. These programs and others have been funded, since 1996, by the federal government's Comprehensive School Reform Demonstration (CSRD) program, to scale up individual school-by-school efforts to national reform models.

THE NEW AMERICAN SCHOOLS EFFORT AND URBAN DISTRICTS

One of the most comprehensive of these efforts was mounted by the New American Schools program (originally the New American Schools Development Corporation). Initiated in 1991 as a component of America 2000, it was defined by then president George H. W. Bush as a business-led effort to

> create a private sector research and development fund of at least $150 million to generate innovation in education. . . . The architects of New American Schools should break the mold. Build for the next century. Reinvent— literally start from scratch and reinvent the American school. No question should be off limits, no answers automatically assumed. We're not after one single solution for every school. We're interested in finding every way to make schools better. (quoted in Glennan, 1998, p. 2)

New American Schools (NAS) started with $40 million and eventually raised more than $150 million to invest in a variety of school-based improvement models. NAS commissioned several reform groups to develop these models, and eight were eventually implemented in more than 550 schools in 26 states.

The RAND Corporation, as Tom Glennan (1998) observed, "played a number of roles ranging from advisor, to field observer, to formal evaluator of the [NAS] effort" (p. III). Through the evaluation reports produced by Glennan and his RAND colleagues, particularly Sue Bodilly (2001), a clear evolution of the NAS effort emerges. NAS started with the assumption that its purpose was to provide new designs for school improvement. The effectiveness of those designs would be assessed by an evaluation probing extent and fidelity of implementation and analyzing student performance results.

This initial conception evolved into a more complex reform. Design teams would develop implementation assistance tailored to targeted schools and would also develop marketing capacities to help schools choose the most appropriate design. Additionally, each design team was encouraged and assisted by NAS to become a self-supporting entity, by charging fees to participating schools and districts. Glennan (1998) argues that through these processes, NAS evolved from a product-development strategy to a venture capitalist strategy.

What is most interesting is the role of the district in this reform. Bodilly's (2001) assessment of the results of the NAS effort indicates that though teachers in participating schools benefited from the professional development the designs offered, test score results did not improve during the 1995–1998 implementation period. Bodilly offers the following explanation for this lack of improvement:

> On average over this period we saw changes in test scores across the different districts that resembled a random pattern. . . . While the design team to school interactions appeared to have some benefit, the interaction between NAS and the districts did not prove fruitful in providing a more supportive environment for teams to work in. Indeed much of this failure might be explained by the heavy reliance of NAS on a relationship with the superintendent. This left little room for building a larger base of support. When the superintendent turned over, as they inevitably did, the new superintendent usually changed reform strategies. Equally problematic was that superintendents often did not use this [NAS design] as the sole reform strategy, thus providing no clear priorities to school staff about reform. But, NAS must also bear some of the blame. It simply did not understand the need for political power and strong district intervention to enable district systemic reform. It lacked the capacity needed to engage the district in real reform. (p. 13)

Thus one of the most comprehensive and well funded of the national school-level reform efforts seems to have foundered on the barrier of limited district capacity. Evaluations of similar school-level reform efforts have come to similar conclusions (see, e.g., Cook et al., 1999). Although many of these school-level improvement efforts have continued to operate through CSRD funding, research has not, in most cases, demonstrated significant success. Instead, as in the NAS evaluation, research has both cited tensions between the national effort and the local district that impeded school-level change and has identified limited district capacity as a key barrier to successful implementation.

The charter school movement, which also began in the early 1990s, is a similar effort to avoid the limitations of district capacity. But as was demonstrated in the previous chapter, charter efforts must reinvent the functions of the district at the school level, primarily by developing support relationships with educational maintenance organizations. Thus, efforts to focus on individual school-by-school reform, whether through CSRD-funded national reform efforts or charters, have not been able to evade the critical role of the district or the limitations of district capacity.

URBAN DISTRICTS AS DRIVERS OF REFORM

In spite of the concentration of school-level CSRD-funded reform efforts, urban districts have not shriveled. Instead, their roles have expanded to include the management of differing school-level interventions. Several big city school systems, for example, required their poorly performing schools to choose one of the nationally certified school-level reform programs to implement, and then supervised that implementation. Other urban districts have mandated which reform programs schools would be required to use. As the 1990s progressed, and the limits of such school-level reform efforts became more apparent, urban systems throughout the country began to shift to more comprehensive district-driven reform. The following case studies focus on three such reform efforts, in New York City's District 2; Kansas City, Kansas; and Hamilton County, Tennessee.

The three districts are very different. The geographic area of District 2 includes most of downtown and midtown Manhattan, from Wall Street and Greenwich Village to Chelsea and Times Square, and the Upper East Side. But though the district serves considerable numbers of advantaged students, more than 50% are students of color and almost 50% are Title I eligible. Kansas City, Kansas, has always been overshadowed by its much larger and more prosperous namesake across the Missouri River. Kansas City is predominantly poor, and its school system faces a constant struggle to raise the resources necessary to serve a predominantly black and Latino student population. Hamilton County includes urban Chattanooga and its suburban and rural surrounding areas. The county's schools serve a broad mix of students: poor students of color in its urban areas, more advantaged suburban students, and working-class and poor white students in its rural areas.

DISTRICT 2'S REFORM EFFORT

Community School District 2 encompasses most of Manhattan south of 95th Street. Anthony Alvarado became the district's superintendent in 1987 and began a major effort to transform the district's teaching and learning practices. The district's student composition is quite varied. Asian students are approximately a third of the district, white students about 32%, Latino students about 21%, and African American students 14%. The district had 46% of its students receiving free or reduced-price lunch in 2005, which placed it in the most advantaged quadrant in a quite impoverished citywide student population. More than 9% of its students use English as a second language (New York City Department of Education, 2005).

Since 1995, District 2's efforts to improve its student achievement have been supported by the Institute for Learning of Pittsburgh University's Learning Research and Development Center (LRDC). The institute enrolls districts in "a program of national seminars and on-site technical assistance designed to help them reorganize as nested learning communities; that is, organizations in which all individuals and units are expected to upgrade their capacities continuously in accord with a shared set of instructional principles and strategies" (Resnick & Glennan, 2002, p. 165).

LRDC carried out a series of studies in District 2, in collaboration with Richard Elmore and Deanna Burney of the Harvard University Graduate School of Education. The following summary of how District 2 restructured itself as a learning organization draws heavily on LRDC's and Elmore and Burney's studies of District 2 (Elmore, 2002; Elmore & Burney, 1997, 1999; Stein & D'Amico, 2002).

Alvarado had previously initiated the choice program in Manhattan's District 4, as analyzed in the previous chapter. In an interview with Elmore, Alvarado described the limitations of the District 4 effort as an overreliance on creative innovators that failed to reach all the district's educators, and an overemphasis on programs rather than on "the broader problem of how to improve teaching and learning across the board. So when I moved to District 2, I was determined to push beyond the District 4 strategy and to focus more broadly on instructional improvement across the board, not just on the creation of alternative programs" (in Elmore & Burney, 1999, p. 267). Alvarado defined the district administration's central purpose in an interview for a 2005 PBS special on urban education reform:

> It is about creating adult learning both on the leadership level and on the teaching level that improves practice that is tied to student learning. Kids learn from teachers. If the kids need to learn more, and more powerfully, then the teachers need to know more, and their teaching has to be more powerful. And the principal has to know how to lead that school to have that improvement in teaching practice occur. ("Interview," 2005, ¶ 43)

Elmore and Burney (1999) argue that the District 2 effort is distinctive because

> [first] it has a specific strategy focused on the improvement of teaching; second, that the strategy has as its goal the sustained improvement of teaching practice . . . ; and third, that the strategy permeates all aspects of the district's organization, including routine management and oversight, budgeting and resource allocation, and district policy. . . . what distinguishes District 2's strategy is that it makes instructional improvement through staff development the central purpose and rationale for the district's role. (p. 288)

A summary of Elmore and Burney's (1999) analysis provides the key components driving District 2's transformation. The district's critical strategies included the following:

- An intense and consistent focus on instruction, which drives a reorganization of all district functions to concentrate on the primacy of teaching and learning
- An understanding and use of the time and complexity involved in changing teachers' and administrators' instructional beliefs and practices
- Sharing teacher and administrator expertise by opening up previously isolated classroom and school practice to observation, visits, walkthroughs, cross-site consultations, demonstrations, and collaborative work
- Focusing on systemwide instructional improvement by targeting specific skills areas—literacy and math, for example—and then ensuring that all the district's practitioners focus improvement efforts on curriculum and teaching practice in those areas
- Recruiting talent and expertise and creating conditions for the collaborative exercise of that talent and expertise in instructional improvement
- Setting clear expectations and decentralizing some responsibility for implementation
- Developing a districtwide culture of collegiality, caring, and respect

Elmore and Burney (1999) also demonstrated how District 2 used professional development to leverage, enhance, and deepen these strategies. The district developed a Professional Development Laboratory that used expert teachers' classrooms for residencies designed to improve teacher classroom practice. The district invested heavily in professional development consultants as coaches, mentors, and guides to improve teacher performance. The district developed varieties of school-level visits, reviews, and walkthroughs to provide consistent support for administrators and classroom teachers. On the basis of findings of these school-level inspection practices, the district initiated and funded off-site and summer training for teachers and administrators in the key content areas of district instructional focus. Finally, the district formed administrator and teacher groupings, and peer networks, to carry out collaborative district work such as the development of new instructional initiatives.

Elmore and Burney (1999) argue that in District 2's practice, these professional development functions are not separable from traditional management functions such as operations, fiscal allocation, personnel, and accountability. The district's administration focused all functions on instruction, and it integrated professional development into administrative intervention and support. This integration, in Elmore and Burney's view, produced the transformation of district practice that not only significantly raised student achievement across the district, but also turned District 2 into a continuously improving learning organization.

Elmore and Burney's analysis identifies a number of key levers that District 2's strategies employed. One of them is time—the time necessary to ensure stability and consistency of focus. Alvarado was the district superintendent for more than 10 years. His deputy superintendent, Elaine Fink, became superintendent after he left the district. Fink's deputy, Shelly Harwayne, became superintendent after Fink's departure.[1] Thus the district enjoyed more than 15 years of consistent leadership focused on the same set of instructional priorities. A District 2 community school board member describes the intensity of that instructional focus:

> As school board members, we were very rarely invited to attend the district principals' conference. But we were asked to come to one focusing on writing and to watch Shelley Harwayne [then a district principal] work with three or four kids. Her ability to assess their writing and figure out the next steps for them to take was breathtaking. Everybody was stunned. We took a break, and Tony [Alvarado] started the next session by saying: "I want to make it crystal clear to you. You cannot sit in this room and be in this district and have any authority in your school if you think you don't have to attain what you just saw. Certainly Shelley is brilliant at what she does. But the district's expectation is that you will learn to be just as brilliant. And your teachers are going to become just as brilliant. I'm not going to accept any excuses that focus on the limitations of the kids. This is the level of performance I expect of you." (H. Doran, personal communication, March 14, 2005)

District 2's reading achievement level ranked it 10th among New York City's 32 community school districts in 1988, at the start of Alvarado's change efforts. Ten years later, the district ranked 2nd in reading citywide, a level it has subsequently sustained. Moreover, according to Alvarado, early in his tenure the district had almost 28% of its students in the bottom quartile of student performance. Alvarado indicated that when he left the district a decade later, only 5% of the district's students were in the bottom quartile ("Interview," 2005).[2]

District 2's effort is one answer to the question raised in Chapter 3 about how accountability can best be integrated into efforts to improve teaching and learning. In terms of Michael Rustin's (2003) definitions of inspection and audit, Alvarado and his colleagues integrated these functions by combining standards and assessments with the supports that schools need to achieve them. District 2 reorganized its administrative operations to focus each school on the primacy of instruction. It set audit standards. It provided the equivalent of traditional English inspection in its visits, reviews, and walkthroughs. Most important, the district provided a set of professional development strategies through which each school's teaching quality could be improved. As Alvarado argues:

> Part of the problem in education is that everybody wants to achieve results, but it is what you have to do to achieve it that people don't know how to do. If you don't focus the organization on learning what to do and you're just hacking people's heads off because the results don't show, you don't improve the quality of learning and the improvement of performance in the system. ("Interview," 2005, ¶ 68)

From my initial chapter's argument that reducing the achievement gap requires restructuring the culture of schooling, to the critical role of inspection in effective accountability, to the limitations of choice programs implemented without adequate support, the critical role of the district has been at the core of this book's analysis. My argument is that the district needs to become the key agent of strategic intervention to transform school-level teaching and learning and improve student performance. District 2's effort is one way that such transformation can be designed and driven by a district administration.

Alvarado and his administrative team accomplished this transformation through a combination of rigorous command-and-control procedures and some decentralization of implementation to the school level. Curriculum and instructional methods in literacy and math, for example, were mandated by the district administration. But through the district's talented budget director, all funding was made fungible so that principals could select the resources that would most effectively drive their schools' instructional improvement. However, principals, teachers, and parents had to accept considerable trade-offs. As a district school board member observed, "Class sizes were very large in District 2. My kids were always in classrooms with 32 other kids. There were no guidance counselors, only the mandated guidance required at the middle school level. And there were no assistant principals" (H. Doran, personal communication, March 14, 2005).

How did District 2's leadership team build the culture of collegiality necessary to transform the district, especially when that transformation imposed a level of privation, in terms of large class sizes and limited guidance and administrative support, on teachers and principals? Alvarado provides an example:

> We won over the membership of the union because what we were doing actually fulfilled their deepest instincts as teachers and as learners. . . . Often we could make momentous decisions on the spot because we absolutely had to have a trust for one another. So the perfect example of this is when we had to improve our school under review, the school selected by the state as not meeting state standards. We decided to create a strategy in June to move into that school a distinguished teacher, a title that did not exist anywhere in the Board of Education. We were going to pay that distinguished teacher $10,000 more [annually]. This is something that sometimes takes years of negotiation. We called the union; we talked about it, and then figured out a way to make it legal and do-able in a way that we could implement it within days—for the opening of the school year. That would never happen in another kind of context. ("Interview," 2005, ¶ 112)

Through strong leadership, training, and support for principals, constant recruitment and development of master teachers, intensive professional development, and a relentless focus on instruction, the district's leadership developed the commitment necessary to transform the district into a continuous learning organization. Teacher union support, especially from the top echelons of city union leadership, was essential. When Alvarado left District 2 to direct instructional improvement throughout the San Diego, California, school system, his inability to develop an equivalent level of teacher union support ultimately limited his effectiveness.

FIRST THINGS FIRST IN KANSAS CITY, KANSAS

The Institute for Research and Reform in Education (IRRE) has been implementing its First Things First (FTF) program in Kansas City, Kansas, since 1996. The Kansas City school district serves 21,000 students; approximately 78% are children of color, and 74% are eligible for free or reduced-price lunches.

FTF began as a collaboration between the IRRE; the school district; and the Ewing Marion Kauffman Foundation, a national foundation based in Kansas City, Missouri (across the Missouri River from Kansas City, Kansas). The foundation initiated the collaboration by inviting the district leadership to an IRRE exploratory session, or roundtable.[3] IRRE designed these roundtables "to present the FTF theory of change by mapping the pathway to long-term outcomes; focusing on the critical features of necessary school reform; and exposing participants to the realities of putting the critical features in place" (Gambone, Klem, Summers, Akey, & Sipe, 2004, p. 10).

After the initial roundtable, the superintendent, the district administration, and the school board agreed to implement FTF. The Kauffman

Foundation encouraged the submission of a proposal to help fund the implementation of FTF. The program was funded and launched in the late fall of 1996, with a series of one-year and then longer-term investments based on meeting the specific benchmarks of a mutual accountability plan developed by the district, IRRE, and the foundation. An executive committee, which included the district's associate superintendent, the president of IRRE, and a Kauffman Foundation senior program officer, was designated to manage the program.

The decision to implement FTF was initially formulated by district leadership without the kind of collaboration or efforts at buy-in that usually characterize reform initiatives. (The district leadership subsequently structured processes to build that buy-in.) But as Steve Gering (2005), the district's deputy superintendent for teaching and learning, indicates:

> Districts [often] wait to implement significant reforms, believing everyone must buy in before doing the work of the reform. This leads to reform burnout before you begin implementation, and many times the end product of this elongated buy-in process is a watered-down reform model with minimal impact. In addition, stretching out the buy-in period allows resisters to rally and possibly sabotage reform efforts. Many well-intentioned reformers never get significant reforms off the ground. (p. 26)

To get the FTF reform off the ground, the district administration made an initial decision that proved to be crucial. The district decided to phase in FTF by introducing it successively to clusters of schools (a cluster consisted of a high school and its feeder middle and elementary schools). The district used most of the 1997 school year to plan the district components of the initiative's implementation. The first cluster began its planning year in 1997–98 and the second cluster in 1998–99; the last two clusters began planning in the 1999–2000 school year.

The original FTF theory of change set out pathways to achieve its ultimate goals—improving youth's educational and developmental outcomes. Given these goals, the theory specifies two intermediate outcomes—providing increased supports and opportunities for students and adults. The theory then defines the processes that will help to produce the intermediate outcomes—initiating change strategies and implementing school-site reforms.

Initiating change strategies was primarily a district function, though both the IRRE and the Kauffman Foundation played key roles. To explain the initiative and to build support for its implementation across the variety of district stakeholders, the district administration structured a series of IRRE roundtables, previously described. These brought together key stakeholders, including the district's teachers union, a National Education

Association (NEA) affiliate, to learn about and ultimately to buy into the FTF program. The district superintendent played a critical role in convening and leading these roundtables and especially in securing the teacher union's support. As Gering (2005) describes it, the partnership between the district and the local NEA made all the difference, creating "a system of support and pressure that kept the district true to its reform plans and kept the local NEA engaged in the process. It was win-win for NEA and for the district" (p. 27).

The district made other major policy and resource decisions that increased the structure, guidance, and support that schools needed to implement the FTF program. The district had already provided a set of instructional and behavioral standards for students. To support FTF, the district did the following:

- Created an instructional framework for all teachers
- Divided the district into clusters for sequential FTF implementation
- Assigned instructional coaches to each school
- Reallocated district staff to schools as school improvement facilitators
- Provided a weekly 2-hour staff development block within school time
- Created executive directors of instruction to help direct and support school-level instructional improvement
- Developed and implemented school walkthroughs to assess whether key FTF components were being implemented[4]
- Gave schools increased authority over hiring and purchasing
- Distributed increasingly sophisticated student performance data by cluster, small learning community, and family advocate group

Superintendent Ray Daniels, appointed in the early years of FTF implementation because he was one of the district administrators most committed to the reform, led the district's efforts to maintain clarity of purpose and consistency of support for the FTF initiative. All parties to the collaboration credit Daniels with the vision and drive necessary to sustain the FTF initiative across time. (Daniels retired in 2004. The new superintendent, Jill Shackelford, has pledged to continue the districtwide reform effort.)

As FTF evolved in the district, the program defined three core goals for implementing school-site reforms: strengthening relationships among students and adults; improving teaching and learning; and reallocating budget, staff, and time to achieve the first two goals. To implement these three core goals, FTF defined seven key components or critical features of school-site reform:

FOR STUDENTS

- Lower student-adult ratios to 15:1 during language arts and math classes.
- Provide continuity of care across the school day, across the school year, and between school and home.
- Set high, clear, and fair standards for what all students should know and be able to do throughout their school careers.
- Provide enriched and diverse learning opportunities so that students become active learners, experience multiple learning modes, link their performance to standards, and be recognized for their achievements.

FOR ADULTS

- Ensure collective responsibility by linking student performance to collective incentives and consequences for small learning communities, schools, and district administrations.
- Provide instructional autonomy and supports by ensuring that day-to-day decisions about teaching are made by teachers at the school site and that they receive the support needed to be effective.
- Ensure flexible allocation of resources by small learning communities and schools so that those resources can best be used to meet students' instructional and developmental needs.

The emphasis on instructional autonomy and supports was eventually redefined as "staff equipped, empowered, and expected to improve instruction" (Quint, Bloom, Black, & Stephens with Akey, 2005, p. 5). The focus on autonomy was reduced and complemented by an insistence on district-level supports and expectations. A School Improvement Facilitator (SIF), assigned to each school by the district administration, became the staff person responsible for implementing these reform components at the school site.

The program currently defines three school-site strategies as critical to accomplishing these reform components: small learning communities, the family advocate system, and instructional improvement. Although the structure of small learning communities evolved as the district's implementation developed, FTF eventually required that all participating schools break down into small learning communities of approximately 250–350 students in secondary schools, with smaller numbers for elementary schools. Secondary school learning communities, or SLCs, are organized on themes and include all the school's grades (6th–8th grade in middle schools, 9th–12th grade in high schools). All SLC teachers have common planning time, approximately 3 hours per week.

The family advocate system was not an initial FTF school-site strategy, but was added in 2001 across the district and in all subsequent FTF sites. All teachers, administrators, and other adults in each school become family advocates for approximately 15–18 students. Each student is paired with a family advocate, and the two meet regularly to assess the student's academic and developmental progress. Each advocate maintains contact with the student's family and helps families support their children's education. In a weekly family advocate period, students meet with their advocate in a group setting. Moreover, during the SLC's common planning time, advocates can communicate with other teachers about their students.

The first district cluster was given the autonomy to plan implementation of the school-level instructional reforms. Although IRRE was increasingly convinced that 4-year (high school), 3-year (middle school) or 6-year (elementary school) vertical SLCs were the most effective structures for providing continuity of care, this SLC pattern only became a requirement for the final two clusters' implementation, once initial gains were recorded in the first cluster of schools. Similarly, though IRRE was convinced that looping in elementary school (the same teachers staying with students across multiple grades) was a powerful intervention for ensuring continuity of care, IRRE and the district did not impose this practice on schools from the outset. Some elementary schools, especially in the first two clusters, interpreted continuity of care to include multiage grouping or team teaching across grade levels, rather than looping. Emerging research on effective implementation of looping in KCK elementary grades helped this practice become a standard for implementation of the districtwide FTF effort.

Because successful implementation of FTF required not only buy-in but also extensive planning and organizing by school staffs, IRRE and the district administration struggled to find the most useful balance between program mandate and school-level initiative. The MDRC evaluation identified a comparable tension when it concluded that "balancing a need for more personalized learning environments with a comprehensive and intensive approach to improving instruction" is the critical task that FTF must accomplish (Quint et al., 2005, p. 8).

IRRE's role was critical to the conception and design phases, as well as to the subsequent processes of implementation. As the MDRC evaluation stresses:

> IRRE came to be viewed as more than an "outside consultant." It offered regular advice to the superintendent and other administrators and became a sounding board for local decisions tied to FTF. IRRE staff visited the district on an

almost monthly basis to monitor the initiative as it unfolded and to provide support to personnel in both the central office and the individual schools . . . IRRE provided the impetus for district officials, SIFs, and others to promulgate standards for high-quality teaching and learning. (Quint et al., 2005, p. 22)

What were the results across 8 years of planning and implementation in Kansas City, Kansas? The district's schools made significant progress in lowering student-adult ratios and providing continuity of care. Student-teacher ratios were reduced in the secondary schools of the two originating clusters without adding teaching staff, through the reallocation of time and personnel. All the district's 12 nonselective secondary schools developed vertical (6–8 or 9–12) SLCs by 2001. Most elementary schools developed 2- or 3-year looping patterns within 3 years of FTF's initiation; all Kansas City, Kansas, elementary schools now use looping.

In terms of instructional improvements, the use of small-group strategies increased significantly in elementary and secondary schools, and student experience of high academic standards increased fourfold. In terms of improvements for adults, collective responsibility seems to have been enhanced in secondary schools. Flexible allocation of resources was accomplished systemwide. SLCs enjoyed clear decision-making authority over space and supplies and participated in schoolwide decisions about budgets and hiring.

The Youth Development Strategies Institute (YDSI) evaluation (2004) found that the FTF implementation produced most of the intermediate results that its theory of change projected. Students perceived teachers as much more supportive at all levels of schooling, and student engagement increased significantly at the secondary level, though less at the elementary level, where engagement had already been high. Although teachers' sense of support from colleagues did not increase, teachers did perceive increased support from the district administration. Moreover, teachers' level of engagement in their work increased in the two initiating clusters.

The FTF theory of change holds that implementation of the core components will produce change in the intermediary outcomes—supports and opportunities for students and adults—that will lead to increased student performance and commitment to learning. Both evaluations found that attendance, and reading and math scores on state testing, improved significantly in elementary and secondary schools. Attendance, for example, rose from 88% at baseline to 94% in 2002–2003 in Kansas City, Kansas, middle schools, and from 77% to 87% across the same time period in high schools. (It was already quite high in elementary schools.) Elementary students went from 29% scoring at proficient or above in 2000–2001 to

47% in 2002–2003 on state reading tests. During the same period, middle school students' scores rose from 36% at proficient or above to 56%, and high school students went from 25% to 34%. Similar though somewhat smaller gains were registered across all school levels in state math testing.[5]

High school graduation rates rose from 57% in 1997–98 to 69% in 2002–2003, and the KCK annual drop-out rate fell from 11% annually to 5% across the same time period. The YDSI evaluation demonstrates significant relationships between the implementation of the core components, the realization of intermediate outcomes, and the increases in student performance that represent the ultimate goals of FTF.

The MDRC evaluation also assessed implementation and outcomes in KCK, and included one more year (2003–2004) of data than the YDSI evaluation.[6] The MDRC findings complement the YDSI results:

> Middle and high schools in Kansas City, Kansas, registered large gains on a wide range of academic outcomes that were sustained over several years and were pervasive across the district's schools; similar gains were not present in the most comparable schools in the state. The improvement occurred over the course of eight years of substantial effort by the school district and by the Institute for Research and Reform in Education (IRRE) to implement FTF as the district's central educational reform. Findings include increased rates of student attendance and graduation, reduced student dropout rates, and improved student performance on the state tests of reading and mathematics. The measured impacts on student test scores reflected double-digit increases in the percentage of students who scored at levels deemed "proficient" by the state and double-digit reductions in the percentage of students scoring at levels deemed "unsatisfactory." (Quint et al., 2005, p. 65)

FTF has also helped to close both race- and class-based achievement gaps in Kansas City, Kansas. Disparities in reading achievement between white and African American students was reduced by 5% from 2001 to 2005, while scores increased significantly for both groups. Similar disparities between white and Latino students were reduced from 21% to 4% in the same period, while scores for both groups significantly increased. The achievement gap between students who did not and students who did receive free and reduced-price lunch also diminished considerably, from 20% in 2001 to 8% in 2005, while both groups' scores rose significantly.

IRRE defines the key lessons from the Kansas City, Kansas, experience: "the importance of working at the district level, what can and can't be left to school choice at the beginning of the reform process, and the critical need to measure both what is being implemented and student outcomes in order to improve them" (quoted in Quint et al., 2005, p. 2). IRRE stresses districtwide reform because it forces all schools, not just those schools choosing a reform program, to be involved. It also ensures that teachers will not be drained away from nonreforming to reforming schools. District reform provides "a coherent focus for district policies [that] compels realignment of core resources to support the highest priorities" (Quint et al., 2005, p. 25).

A districtwide focus enables the Kansas City, Kansas, district to provide systemic professional development, personnel, budgeting, and accountability policies designed to support the initiative. Districtwide reform also helps to assure continuity and sustainability. "When the reform initiative becomes the work of the district rather than a program in one or a few schools, it is less likely to be influenced by changes in school or district leadership or even shifting state policies" (Quint et al., 2005, p. 26). FTF in the Kansas City, Kansas, district has experienced four different superintendents and several major changes in state policy while managing a steady increase in improvement across a decade of reform effort.

DISTRICT-LEVEL REFORM IN HAMILTON COUNTY, TENNESSEE

A strong partnership between the district and a school reform intermediary organization drove district-level change in Kansas City, Kansas. In contrast, district-level change evolved in Hamilton County, Tennessee, through a series of local and national partnerships coordinated by the vision and collaborative skills of an entrepreneurial superintendent.

Hamilton County surrounds and includes Chattanooga, Tennessee's fourth largest city. In 1994, a majority of the city's voters forced the merger of the Chattanooga city schools and the Hamilton County school system into one consolidated unit.[7] The two systems were very different. Chattanooga's schools served a mostly urban population with an inner-city core of poor black parents. The school system had a 64% African American student population, and almost 60% of its students were eligible for free and reduced-price lunch. Hamilton County, in contrast, served mostly suburban and rural areas. Only 20% of its students were eligible for subsidized school lunches, and less than 5% were African American.

Predictably, student achievement in the county schools was consistently higher than the city's. But both systems lost significant numbers of students to Chattanooga's flourishing private school sector. Estimates are that almost 30% of the county's age-eligible students were annually enrolled in private schools.

Chattanooga's highly developed foundation sector, led by the Lyndhurst Foundation, had played a critical role in the transformation of the city's downtown and riverfront in the 1980s and early 1990s. That sector also created and continued to invest in a large and very effective Public Education Foundation (PEF), initially established in 1988. The PEF's first director, Steven Prigohzy, had been the initiating principal of a highly effective Chattanooga magnet high school that had evolved into a K–12 school of choice.

After the merger vote, the Hamilton County School Board asked the PEF to help frame a vision for the new consolidated school system. The PEF appointed a Planning Committee, representing educational, business, civic, and community leadership, to develop a mission statement and a framework for the new system. After 7 months of meetings; research; visits to other city systems, including to New York City's new small schools; and consultation with a wide range of experts, the Planning Committee presented its report to the Hamilton County School Board in February 1996.

The report recommended a standards-based accountability system, increased efforts at both preschool education and school-to-work transition; substantial autonomy for schools, combined with increased parental roles in decision making; and school configurations that closely connected schools to their students, parents, and the surrounding community. The report argued that smaller classes and smaller schools, comprehensive professional development, and increased funding were critical to implementing these recommendations. (The Planning Committee's emphasis on the need for more funding would become particularly prophetic across the ensuing decade.)

The Hamilton County School Board accepted the Planning Committee's report and appointed Dr. Jesse Register, who had overseen two previous mergers in North Carolina, to lead the newly consolidated school district. Register began his work early in 1997, and in July that year the two school systems officially merged. Register faced major challenges. Many county commissioners, educators, and residents were unhappy about the necessity to take on predominantly African American schools. They perceived those schools as poorly performing, their students as less academically capable than county students, and their parents as uncommitted to quality education for their children. They also felt that the city schools enjoyed an overallocation of scarce fiscal resources such as Title I funds.

Many of Chattanooga's African American parents and citizens, in contrast, perceived county schools and the educators who staffed them as hostile to their children and uncommitted to providing them a quality education. These differing perceptions, based on differing experiences of education and race, created significant tensions throughout the early merger years. Although somewhat abated, these tensions still shape leadership and constituency responses to equity concerns, school improvement policies, and funding issues throughout the city and the county.

Register's task was somewhat eased by two major accomplishments. The PEF had secured a substantial Annenberg Foundation Challenge grant in 1995 to aid the creation of the new district. And the city and county unions, both affiliates of the National Education Association (NEA), had combined into a single union after a year's effort to integrate associations with potentially conflicting bargaining styles.

Register's first moves signaled his dual strategies—improve teaching and learning and increase integration. Using funding from the Annenberg Foundation Challenge grant, and working with the PEF, Register structured an 18-month process of developing the district's academic standards by involving more than 300 teachers across the county in writing them. The resulting standards were informed by national work, but were also rooted in local curriculum and instruction. The teachers who led the standards effort encouraged the acceptance and use of the standards across the county's schools. Most critical, the process created one set of standards for all the system's students, city and county.

Register also chose approximately 40 of his curriculum and instructional supervisors to be Consulting Teachers, and he moved them from administrative offices to frontline school roles. The CTs, as they came to be known, developed into essential school-site coaches charged with improving instruction and facilitating school improvement throughout the system.

Using a federal grant, Register initiated a magnet school program to draw black students into selected county schools and to attract white students into selected inner-city Chattanooga schools. This magnet strategy subsequently merged with foundation, corporate, and university efforts to expand downtown revitalization and generate center-city housing development that would attract middle-income families.[8] Register also redrew school-zone boundaries to increase integration in several schools serving border areas between predominantly black and white neighborhoods, although Hamilton County was not subject to any court-ordered desegregation mandate.

As these changes developed, Register began working intensively with the PEF and its new leader, Dan Challener. Using Annenberg Foundation funds, and working with a national expert, the two developed the Hamilton County Leadership Institute to identify, recruit, train, and support new leaders for the county's schools. The Leadership Institute began operating in 1999 and was housed in the PEF's offices. The work of the Leadership Institute led to an invitation from the Carnegie Corporation to compete for a grant for high school reform. In 2001, the district and the PEF collaborated on a proposal to Carnegie to transform the county's 17 high schools. The proposal was accepted, and Carnegie allocated $8 million across 5 years to Hamilton County to implement the foundation's Schools for a New Society (SNS) effort. (The PEF raised an additional $6 million, primarily from local foundations, including Lyndhurst, and the district redeployed $2 million in system funds to meet Carnegie's 1:1 match requirement.)

During the SNS planning period, the district and PEF encouraged all 17 district high schools to write individual plans that developed each school's unique pathway to change.[9] But the district and PEF also required all high schools to base their plans on four core strategies: increasing teacher quality, personalizing instruction, increasing academic rigor, and creating more flexible opportunities to learn. The district and PEF set the following goals for all the county's high schools:

- Ninety-five percent of 9th grade students would move to 10th grade in one year.
- Ninety-five percent of all students would pass the Tennessee-required Gateway exams in major subjects.
- Ninety-five percent of entering students would graduate from high school.
- The percentage of students taking remedial courses in area colleges would be reduced by 75%.

The initiative's combination of decentralized planning and implementation, structured by strong central guidelines, characterizes Register's leadership style. But it also responds to the differing histories, community contexts, and educational philosophies of the district's mix of schools—urban, suburban, and rural. (The county is more than 50 miles wide and encompasses dozens of different communities.) Register's management of the consolidated district has stressed the strength of its diversity and its individual schools' capacity for improvement. But Register has intervened whenever he felt the necessity for strong centralized direction.

An example is his mandate that all high schools offer a universal college-bound curriculum and that high school graduation require students to complete a course of study including multiple years of English, math, social studies, and science, as well as a foreign language. Observing the development of the SNS high school initiative, Register grew increasingly convinced that the drive for academic rigor needed a higher bar. Given the collapse of manufacturing in Hamilton County, and an increasingly skills-driven regional economy in which insurance, health care, computer management, and systems analysis firms were becoming the dominant industries, Register shared the national concerns about the limitations of traditional vocational curricula. His single-path curriculum, as it came to be called, did not assume that all Hamilton County graduates would attend college. But single path did assume that all Hamilton County graduates needed to successfully complete a curriculum that would prepare them for college or the demands of sophisticated workplaces.

Register and Sheila Young, the deputy superintendent of secondary schools for the Hamilton County Department of Education (HCDE), traveled the county presenting arguments for single path. They met with parent groups, business leaders, churches, civic associations, and volunteer organizations. Neither Register's administration nor the SNS initiative had developed a strong community-engagement component, but Register and Young's efforts began to change that. They mobilized a base of support for single path that overcame limited but persistent opposition.

Opposition came from some suburban high schools, for example, that feared the watering down of traditional college prep sequences. Others opposed the idea that all students needed algebra and chemistry. But Register and his colleagues convinced most of the county's constituencies of the necessity for single path. The consensus they built became the platform for a broader base when the district was forced to mobilize support for a budget increase a few years later.

At this writing, Hamilton County's participation in the Carnegie Corporation's Schools for a New Society (SNS) high school restructuring initiative is entering its final year. Under the leadership of Bill Kennedy, former principal of the district's first magnet high school, and Warren Hill, the HCDE Director of High Schools, all the county's high schools have been substantially restructured. Most have developed thematic academies and other small learning communities, pre-ninth-grade summer school and transition programs, new forms of advisories for counseling and support, schoolwide literacy curricula, and teacher teams who meet constantly to assess progress and plan improvements. Most important, not only at the high schools but across the district, administrators and teachers are studying varieties of school- and student-level data to analyze their school's accomplishments, identify their school's instructional needs, and make the necessary improvements.

This emphasis on data-driven improvement began when Register created a Data and Accountability Division soon after he became superintendent in 1997 and charged it with producing disaggregated data for district, school, and classroom use. The drive for data-based improvement was aided by the PEF, which created its own data capacity and augmented the district's production, dissemination, and analysis of school-useful data. The district's high schools, for example, worked for almost 2 years to develop a definition of what constitutes a 10th grader, so that every school could accurately calculate the percentage of students who move from 9th to 10th grade in any given year. Now any principal can easily produce that percentage, and all the district's high school principals use the same procedure and reliable numbers to calculate it.

This stress on providing the critical data for school improvement exemplifies the district's balancing act between school-based planning and district mandate. Challener's (2004) view of the SNS planning process is indicative:

> While we did not mandate a model, we did require all schools to gather and review an immense amount of data, including survey data from all ten thousand of our high school students. Schools were given a full year to review their data, learn about best practices, talk among themselves, and travel to high-performing high schools in different parts of the nation. Most importantly, each school's staff was given time to construct its plan: monthly meeting time, four full professional days, four half days, and a weekend retreat.
>
> Because each school constructed its own plan, the blueprint for change has become part of each school's daily work. When you walk into most schools, you'll meet passionate advocates for the changes. It's their plan, and they own it. Indeed, most of our high schools have developed themed academies, and almost all have implemented a literacy program. But they did this based on what their students said, what their data said, and what their teachers said—not because the superintendent mandated it. By trusting each school and allowing for dialogue and critical inquiry, we created momentum and commitment usually absent from most high school reform efforts. (p. 77)

Anthony Bryk and Barbara Schneider's *Trust in Schools* (2002) analyzes the critical role of trust among teachers, parents, and administrators in building the school-level relationships that support successful teaching and learning. But little has been written about how district administrations build the trust necessary to sustain districtwide support for school-level improvement. Developing such trust requires reciprocal relationships: district administrators must trust the capacity and commitment of school principals and staffs to design and implement the improvement initiative. School-level practitioners must trust the capacity and commitment of district-level staff to support and sustain their efforts and to provide critical leadership interventions. The Hamilton County district has begun to learn how to build such reciprocal trust. Consider the following examples.

Early in the SNS initiative, the high school principals balked at the scale of change the SNS reform demanded. "We're not going out on a limb," several of them told the Carnegie Corporation's program officer in charge of the SNS effort, "until we're convinced that the superintendent and the district administration will support us." What would convince them? More access to the superintendent and his cabinet, because the high school principals felt isolated from the rest of the district and removed from the administrative chain of command. And more structured participation in decision making, because the principals feared they wouldn't be able to define and secure the changes in district policy necessary to support and sustain the SNS initiative.

Register responded by appointing a new director for high schools, initiating regular meetings with the high school principals, and convening periodic cabinet meetings with representatives of those principals to identify necessary policy changes. As a result, the high school principals have contributed to major changes in district personnel, transportation, student assignment, and fiscal policy and have become more confident that the district will support their school-level initiatives. The necessary levels of reciprocal trust began to develop.[10]

More recently, the district collaborated with the PEF, several local foundations, and New York University's Institute for Education and Social Policy (IESP) to initiate a middle school improvement program. IESP produced a report that analyzed a wide range of middle school outcomes and recommended the core components of a districtwide middle school improvement program. To help initiate the program, the district wanted each school to study the school-level data IESP's report provided. But because the data was arrayed in rank order, the district was reluctant to distribute it. Administrators didn't want to embarrass schools by subjecting them to public exposure through the rankings.

The superintendent suggested the solution: Give each school their own data, but don't identify any other school's data. The tables that were ultimately disseminated were specially configured for each school. They showed each school's results and its rank (high, middle, or low) in the districtwide distribution for every indicator. But each school received only its own results; no school was privy to another's. Thus all the district's middle schools could analyze the relative level of their achievement on a wide range of critical indicators, without risking embarrassing exposure. A new districtwide improvement program began with an initial basis of trust.

A final example: Early in Register's tenure, his efforts to improve teaching quality hit a barrier of union resistance when he attempted to change the district's teacher-transfer policy. After several difficult sessions with the union leadership, Register changed strategies and approached the leadership with a proposal to try collaborative bargaining. The union leadership, aided by the state NEA affiliate, assimilated the components of that collaborative bargaining approach:

> Once the union and the district began collaborative bargaining—the union making its concerns clear, and the district sharing the problems it needed to solve—the union became part of the decision-making process and began working with the district administration to find mutually acceptable solutions to challenges confronting the system. (Foster, 2005, pp. 2–3)

What followed was a negotiated teacher-transfer policy that gave Register the flexibility to assign experienced teachers to the schools that needed them most. "Placing a high level of importance on faculty [has caused] a huge turnaround in quality," Register observed (Esposito, 2005).

Register's ability to forge a collaborative, trust-based relationship with the teachers union proved critical to yet another district-foundation-PEF effort, the Benwood initiative. The Benwood Foundation, a local philanthropy, commissioned the PEF to design and implement an improvement program targeting Chattanooga's nine inner-city elementary schools. Several of these schools were among the most poorly performing in the state. The foundation granted $5 million across 5 years for the improvement effort, with another $2.5 to be raised by PEF. The district and PEF designed an intensive focus on improving classroom instruction through a universal-literacy curriculum, extensive professional development, coaches for new teachers, and reading specialists for struggling students. Led by veteran educator Stephanie Spencer and supported by Ray Swafford, HCDE's Assistant Superintendent for Urban Schools, the Benwood initiative set rigorous standards that drove a demanding improvement campaign.

When the district identified teachers in what came to be called the Benwood schools who were not performing effectively, the district and the teachers union cooperated in transferring those teachers to other district schools where they could get the support they needed. The district, the union, and PEF structured an incentive program to attract new young teachers and retain effective veteran teachers at the Benwood schools. Chattanooga's mayor organized a business and civic alliance to provide further incentives to recruit, support, and sustain teachers in those schools. Among the incentives are individual and school-level bonuses, mortgage assistance, and free tuition to enroll in a master's program for urban teachers, developed at the University of Tennessee–Chattanooga, through a grant provided by yet another local foundation.

What are the results of the Benwood and Carnegie initiatives in the nine low-performing elementary schools and the 17 county high schools? The Benwood schools have made striking gains in reading and math achievement across the past 4 years. On the state's 2005 reading/language arts testing, the Benwood schools' scores have increased by almost 20%, to 77.1% at proficient or advanced levels, since 2003, and almost 16%, to 70.7%

proficient or advanced on the state's math testing. The achievement gap in reading/language arts between the Benwood schools and all the district's other elementary schools has narrowed from 26.4% to 15.5% in the same period. (The district administration and the PEF are currently planning to extend the Benwood initiative to all the county's elementary schools.)

At the high school level, graduation rates have increased across the county, and the dropout rates have correspondingly diminished. The annual ACT scores of Hamilton County's high school students have increased in most of the past 5 years, have topped the statewide average, and are approaching the national average. The percentage of Hamilton County graduates in the remedial courses of the area's colleges has steadily declined, while an increasing percentage of the district's graduates are enrolling in college.

At both the elementary and high school levels, state testing results have improved every year, and all the district's schools registered huge increases in the 2005 testing outcomes. Hamilton County results exceeded the state average and the average of the state's urban districts by a good margin in almost every subject at every grade level. Moreover, the achievement gap in testing outcomes between black and white students has narrowed each year for the past 4 years (2001–2005). Finally, the trend of increasing enrollment losses to the county's private schools has flattened out; the district is no longer losing significant numbers of students.

These results have been accomplished in a context of severe fiscal scarcity. Tennessee is a very low tax state that provides relatively little funding to its public schools; it ranked 45th out of all the states in total expenditures per pupil in 2001–2002 (National Center for Education Statistics, 2002). Moreover, the state's fiscal allocation formulas privilege suburban districts and disadvantage urban districts. Worse, though the county board of education governs the schools, the county board of commissioners, the county's governing body, provides the finances.

The County Commission, dominated by a conservative suburban and rural faction, refused for successive years to grant funding increases for the district's critical schooling needs. The county's teachers, for example, have received only the state-mandated minimum salary for the past 5 years, while surrounding Tennessee districts were increasing salaries, particularly for beginning teachers. Stung by the superintendent's criticism of the commission's refusal to vote for district funding increases, several commissioners embarked on a campaign to denigrate the school system and its leadership. They charged the superintendent with inefficient fiscal management, maintaining a bloated central administration, and producing persistently poor student outcomes. Although these charges were demonstrably false, the commissioners used them to mount a mud-slinging attack against the superintendent and organized a majority of commissioners to continue to reject desperately needed school system budget increases.

The superintendent and his cabinet, aided by supporters in the business and civic community, began a counterattack to document the falseness of the commission members' charges and to publicize the increases in student academic achievement that the district's reforms had produced. The base of support Register had built during the single-path-curriculum debate, the formation of a districtwide Parent Advisory Council, the support of the teachers union, and a consistent flow of media stories that focused on the district's achievements, began to turn the tide. A few weeks after the huge gains in state 2005 testing were reported, the County Commission voted, five to four, to pass a tax increase allocating critically needed millions of new dollars to the Hamilton County school system.

But the years of attacks on the superintendent's leadership have taken a toll. Register became convinced that his accumulated baggage as the lightning rod for conservative opposition limited his leadership potential. To clear the way for a new accommodation with city and county leadership, Register announced his resignation a few weeks after the vote for the tax increase. In his statement he expressed his conviction that new leadership would steer the district to new heights of student achievement.

Register had been the Hamilton County superintendent for almost 10 years, and his administrative team was remarkably stable. This stability, combined with Register's consistency of purpose, provided a steady platform for innovation and improvement. Through the collaborations between the district and PEF, a series of innovative foundation-funded programs brought new conceptual energy, new resources, and critical incentives to the district. Register initiated and then refined a simultaneous bottom-up and top-down strategy to develop and guide that innovation. His ability to build the levels of reciprocal trust necessary to support and sustain that innovation have transformed school and district practice in Hamilton County schools and produced steadily accelerating gains in student achievement.

Late in Register's tenure, the County Commission invited the Annenberg Institute for School Reform (AISR) to conduct a review of the school system's operations and assess the role and effectiveness of the central office. The recommendations of AISR's Central Office Review for Results and Equity (CORRE) team suggest both the dimensions of the Hamilton County school system's achievements and the directions for further improvement:

- Deepen and sustain the focus on increasing instructional quality.
- Increase transparency and effectiveness of central office decision making.

- Use data to broaden access to information about student and school performance.
- Improve the targeting of resources to meet student needs.
- Improve communication about the district's achievements, priorities, and needs.
- Increase community accountability for public education.
- Define and focus on how all the county's constituencies can join forces to support their public schools.

COMMON ELEMENTS OF DISTRICT-LEVEL REFORM

What are the commonalties across the three very different efforts to implement district-driven improvement described in this chapter? First, all three districts were led by superintendents who initiated, supported, and sustained reform for at least a decade.[11] This leadership stability provided consistent administrative direction and commitment, as well as the time scale necessary to successfully implement districtwide reform.

Although the case studies do not focus on the role of each district's school board, the three districts' leadership stability demonstrates their school boards' clarity, cohesion, and commitment to reform. School board members maintained their support for their superintendents' reform visions and were not deterred by the difficulties of implementing complex districtwide reform strategies. Without strong and stable school board support, superintendents cannot sustain the momentum, energy, and commitment necessary to transform districts. As Steve Gering (2005), deputy superintendent for teaching and learning for the Kansas City, Kansas, public schools concludes,

> Long-term continuity of leadership has been critical to the success and longevity of the work in KCKPS [the Kansas City, Kansas, public schools]. Even though there have been four different individuals sitting in the superintendent's chair, the focus on the reform has not wavered. This is a tribute to the leadership role the board of education has played in this work. (p. 28)

Second, all three districts structured their districtwide strategies to focus on improving instruction. The administrative, structural, governance, budget, curricular, and personnel changes each district designed and implemented were focused on supporting and improving instruction. Each district's reform effort was focused on changing instructional practice as the critical priority.

Third, all three district reforms either began as, or eventually moved toward, universal efforts that involved all the district's schools. As Steve Gering (2005) indicates,

> KCKPS's approach to reform was based on the premise that the entire school district needed improvement. To realize this, all schools, pre-K through 12, participated in the reform, along with central staff. Staff members across the system, across grade levels, and across sites were able to discuss reform principles using a common language, resulting in a sense of collective responsibility for all the students. (p. 23)

Fourth, all three districts developed collaborative relationships with their teacher unions that involved those unions as key players in and supporters of the reform. Without that support, the reforms could not have achieved or sustained their effectiveness.

Fifth, all three districts developed and sustained strong external partnerships that provided significant definition, direction, and support for their reforms. The Learning Research and Development Center in District 2, the Institute for Research and Reform in Education in Kansas City, and the Public Education Foundation in Hamilton County became key collaborative partners in each reform effort.

Sixth, each district's reform worked to find the most appropriate balance between district mandate and school-level decisions. District 2 made resource decisions a school-level prerogative. Kansas City gave schools the responsibility to make key instructional decisions. Hamilton County's high school initiative started with school-level planning. But in each case, the district made the critical, nonnegotiable decisions that structured their overall reforms. Finding the right balance between district direction and school-level implementation proved critical to the success of each reform effort.

Seventh, each district's reform developed new forms of collaborative leadership in efforts to make the reform a collective responsibility, rather than simply a leadership initiative. The peer learning networks in District 2, the cluster and small learning community leadership teams in Kansas City, and the principals' networks and the Critical Leadership Group (see note 10) in Hamilton County all represent new forms of shared leadership that developed to more effectively carry out the work of reform.

Finally, all three districts invested significant resources in professional development efforts to improve the quality of teaching. Analysis of each district's budget across the reform years would demonstrate increasing percentages of overall district resources committed to professional development to improve the performance of the district's teachers.

These three systemic reform efforts are not the only examples of successful district-driven improvement. Many other districts are developing similar change strategies to improve their teaching and learning.[12] The next phase of school reform will increasingly be districtwide initiatives driven by administrations committed to universal, comprehensive, and sustained efforts to improve student achievement.

Organizing for Effective Schools and Districts

Deep, fundamental change will only come when those in these poor regions raise their voice and work for change.
—Cynthia M. Duncan, PBS interview

IN 1991, New York City Schools Chancellor Joseph Fernandez issued *Children of the Rainbow,* a multicultural curriculum guide for the city's first-grade teachers. The guide's aim was straightforward: to "enable teachers to plan for children from the start to reach their potential without developing stereotypical notions based on race, sex, religion, color, national origin, handicapping conditions, or sexual orientation" (*Children of the Rainbow,* 1991). The Rainbow guide was designed to enrich students' understanding of the diversity of the city's cultures, to help make education more effective throughout the school system. A few pages discussed the need for teacher sensitivity to students who were children of gay or lesbian parents, suggesting that teachers

> should include references to lesbians/gay people in all curricular areas and should avoid exclusionary practices by presuming a person's sexual orientation, reinforcing stereotypes, or speaking of lesbians/gays as "they" or "other."
>
> If teachers do not discuss lesbian/gay issues, they are not likely to come up. Children need actual experiences via creative play, books, visitors etc. in order for them to view lesbians/gays as real people to be respected and appreciated. Educators have the potential to help increase the tolerance and acceptance of the lesbian/gay community and to decrease the staggering number of hate crimes perpetrated against them. (p. 372)

Children of the Rainbow listed, among hundreds of titles in the Appendix, *Heather Has Two Mommies* and *Jennie Lives with Eric and Martin* as books teachers might use for supplementary classroom reading to heighten children's understanding.

The school system was already embroiled in another episode of the city's ongoing culture wars, because the Fernandez regime had instituted a K–12 HIV-AIDS curriculum, and had begun a condom-distribution program in the city's high schools. The release of the Rainbow curriculum guide set off a renewed firestorm of outrage and protest. Conservative religious leaders charged that the school system was legitimating homosexuality and encouraging deviant sexual proselytizing in the city's classrooms. Conservative political organizations such as the Christian Coalition argued that the school system was promoting immorality and sin by treating homosexuality and lesbianism as acceptable lifestyles. The controversy quickly became intense, inflammatory, and abusive, as critics and defenders of *Children of the Rainbow* traded accusations of homophobia, promiscuity, bigotry, and pedophilia.

Traditionally, under New York City's semidecentralized system, curriculum guides were notoriously underused; such guides often languished on library and classroom shelves in community school districts. But after Community School Board 24 in Queens voted its disapproval of the guide and refused to authorize its use, Chancellor Fernandez mandated the use of *Children of the Rainbow* and ordered all the city's community school boards to approve it. When the District 24 School Board refused to rescind its disapproval, the chancellor removed the board and replaced it with his own appointees.

Waves of opposition targeted the chancellor and the central board of education. Busloads of protestors descended on 110 Livingston Street, the school system's headquarters in Brooklyn, to inveigh against the chancellor and the *Children of the Rainbow*. Newspapers, TV, and talk radio were consumed with charges, countercharges, and inflammatory debate. In community school districts throughout the city, normal business was suspended as parents and community members demanded that their school boards affirm or reject the use of the Rainbow curriculum. And in my school district, hundreds of concerned parents attended a school board meeting to demand that we take a stand on the *Children of the Rainbow*.

When our board reviewed the few sections of the curriculum that had provoked the outpouring of opposition, we realized how deeply we were divided. Several board members strongly supported the curriculum's effort to demystify gay and lesbian families and encourage sensitivity to and acceptance of their children. But other board members who had long believed that sex education usurped parental responsibilities were fervently opposed to classroom discussions about homosexuality. One board member argued that defining homosexuality as a lifestyle and a culture represented the domestication of sin and the triumph of the gay and lesbian agenda to subvert traditional American culture. Several board members felt that first grade was too early to introduce any notion of sexuality.

Our discussion was deeply troubling but not polarizing. Members struggled to articulate their beliefs and probe the views of others because we understood the difficulties of the task before us. We all agreed that the curriculum guide had stirred up such passion that we needed to hear and consider the views of parents and community members across the district before we reached our decision. So we scheduled a series of special hearings and invited our district's parents and community members to discuss whether our school board should approve or reject the Children of the Rainbow curriculum.

Our public meetings had always been open to parent and citizen input. We rotated our meetings across the district's schools. Anyone could speak; no advance sign-up was required. Simultaneous translation in Spanish was always provided, since our district's student body was approximately 60% Latino. Except when a particular issue generated a large press of speakers, we set no time limits. Attendance by 50 to 100 parents and community members was fairly standard, and the local press was always present.

Still, we were unprepared for the resulting outpouring. More than 500 parents attended our first special meeting, and almost 1,000 parents came to each of the following two. Our school board was convinced we could maintain order without the need for security. But our superintendent was not as confident and arranged for a discreet police presence.

Large numbers of parents and community members, including many gay and lesbian residents of our district, vigorously supported the use of the Rainbow curriculum and argued for the need to make the district's classrooms hospitable to the children of gay and lesbian families. Several evangelical and Pentecostal churches in the predominantly Latino neighborhoods of our district strongly opposed the curriculum, and they were supported by a citywide effort to unify such churches against the curriculum's use. Thus there was potential for heated confrontation at every meeting.

As president of the board I had to gavel down interruptions, appeal for order, and admonish speakers who refused to observe their time limits or attempted to rally the audience. A few times I had to threaten to cut off the microphone or suspend the hearings. Although there were many angry outbursts, there were relatively few direct confrontations, and no violence. The police were vigilant but not obtrusive.

At each meeting, several speakers expressed blatant and sometime vicious homophobia. But there were also repeated expressions of support for gays and lesbians from the Rainbow curriculum's opponents. Many speakers began their statements with a disavowal of bigotry, declaring that "my sister-in-law is a lesbian" or "my cousin is gay," before defining their opposition to the Rainbow curriculum. Intense religious conviction motivated much of the opposition. "First you took away our Bibles and our prayers," one young Latino father yelled at us. "Then you took away our right to discipline our children. Now you want to take away our right to teach them about sex according to our own beliefs."

As the hearings continued, our school board discussions intensified, and the pressure on us to reach a decision mounted. We finally reached a compromise that exemplified our board's style. We would affirm the *Children of the Rainbow*'s use throughout our district, but we would omit any specific references to sexuality in the first grade. Moreover, the Rainbow curriculum's use in each school would be determined by consultations with the school's parent body. We also affirmed the use of the multicultural curriculum guides our district had previously developed, which the Rainbow curriculum had built on.

At our regular monthly meeting after the series of special hearings, our board voted seven to one, with one abstention, to affirm the Rainbow curriculum. There were boos, hisses, and applause from members of the audience, but no outpouring of anger (though as a precaution, police officers accompanied all the board members to our cars). What I sensed, walking through the crowd after the meeting ended, was an odd catharsis— a mix of exhaustion and relief that the issue had finally been decided.

The citywide resolution was far more polarized. Faced with continuing waves of confrontation, the central school board voted to dismiss Chancellor Fernandez and to rescind his suspension of Community School Board 24. The citywide anger receded quickly after Fernandez's dismissal. By the time Ramon Cortines was selected as the next city schools chancellor, the Children of the Rainbow curriculum had become a peripheral issue.

The aftermath differed in my district. The Rainbow conflict coalesced both supporters and opponents in the constituency organizing for the upcoming school board election. Although the curriculum's foes had threatened to defeat our pro-Rainbow school board, a slate of six proponents of the Rainbow curriculum, led by a charismatic lesbian lawyer, overwhelmed the opposition. Thus the legacy of the curriculum wars in our district was an affirmation of the Rainbow curriculum's support for the children of gay and lesbian parents.

At the core of this epic conflict was the issue of the just treatment of such children in the city's schools. Rainbow proponents argued that just treatment, as well as effective education, required legitimating the parenting arrangements, and by implication the sexual orientations, of the children of gay and lesbian families. Moreover, legitimation meant that teachers should accept those family arrangements and sexual orientations as equivalent to traditional family arrangements and traditional sexuality.

For Rainbow opponents, the just treatment of children of gay and lesbian couples in public school classrooms was not possible if such treatment involved acceptance of forms of sexuality they defined as immoral and sinful. In their perception, such legitimation sanctioned the teaching of deviant sexuality to their own and other people's children.

In *Democratic Education,* Amy Gutmann (1987) argues that such fundamental conflicts are the basis for what she calls

> a democratic theory of education, which makes a democratic virtue out of our inevitable disagreement over educational problems. The democratic virtue, too simply stated, is that we can publicly debate educational problems in a way much more likely to increase our understanding of education and each other. . . . The policies that result from our democratic deliberations will not always be the right ones, but they will be more enlightened—by the values and concerns of the many communities that constitute a democracy—than those that would be made by unaccountable educational experts. (p. 11)

Our school board did not initiate the Rainbow curriculum hearings to advance the quality of our district's educational decision making. We were on the spot; passions were rising throughout the district, and we would have to decide the issue. We thought a public dialogue would encourage the airing of a broad range of opinions and beliefs, reduce hostilities, and lower the district's collective temperature. Yet as our hearings progressed, I sensed that we were involved in a more complex process of discussion and debate that approached the kind of democratic deliberation that Gutmann espouses.

How did this happen? Partisans on each side of the issue were forced to listen to, and perhaps even to entertain, arguments they had not previously considered. Opponents had to deal with one another as real people rather than as stereotypes or symbols. Uncomfortable realities were articulated. "My daughter never talks about us in school," a lesbian mother testified. "She won't reveal that she has two mothers because she's ashamed, because she's afraid of being teased or bullied. Would you want your daughter to be ashamed of her parents in school?" Another mother responded that she was not opposed to making classrooms places where the children of gay and lesbian couples could feel at home. "I just don't want sexuality to come into it. Our schools shouldn't be teaching kids about sexuality, whether it's straight or gay. And certainly not in first grade."

The hearing formats were not ideal for democratic dialogue. Participants addressed us, as board members, rather than addressing one another, because we would, ultimately, decide the issue. Moreover, we scheduled the hearings as large public debates, set the ground rules, and controlled the terms and time limits of public participation. Still, in spite of the angry attacks and the vituperative denunciations, it was clear that people wanted to testify, debate one another, and hear ideas that they opposed. We adjourned one hearing well after 2:00 A.M., and knots of people throughout the auditorium continued talking, arguing, and debating. Watching intense conversations develop throughout the hearings, I wondered if the dialogue was helping to raise the levels of understanding about the complexities of the issue and the difficulties of a just solution.

Our school board experienced a similar process; the districtwide hearings elevated our deliberations and pushed us toward a decision that tried to honor what we heard. To reach a consensus that was almost unanimous, each of us gave considerable ground from our original positions. But almost all of us felt that the decision we fashioned was just.

Gutmann's (1987) theory of democratic education holds that because such epic conflicts are inevitable in public education, we should strive to resolve them through direct forms of dialogue. Gutmann defines public education's ultimate purpose as the development of a citizenry adept at making such schooling decisions (and by extension, all key societal decisions) through participatory dialogue. Her answer to the question, What is education for? is that ultimately education should shape the process of "conscious social reproduction—the ways in which citizens are or should be empowered to influence the education that in turn shapes the political values, attitudes and modes of behavior of future citizens" (p. 14).

Thus, for Gutmann, democratic education's ultimate purpose is to produce democratic education. But her vision of how democratic education can contribute to conscious social reproduction does not clearly address fundamental power disparities. Although Gutmann acknowledges such disparities, her theory does not focus on how they can be successfully challenged. Yet it is precisely the disparities in power between advantaged and disadvantaged communities that limit the possibilities for the kind of democratic education Gutmann envisions. Equal access to dialogue depends on equivalent power. As long as urban elites can structure and limit participation in decision making, such power imbalances prevent or pervert genuinely democratic dialogue. For democratic education to become a reality, the capacity to successfully challenge existing power must be factored into the theory.

Consider, from this perspective, how the Rainbow conflict played out in my district. Our school board was composed of seven whites and two Latinos, in a school district that was approximately 60% Latino, 20% white, 15% African American and 5% Asian American. Thus the distribution of the political, social, and financial capital critical to the constituency organizing that results in election to the school board clearly favored white neighborhoods and worked against communities of color. Several of us as board members were committed to reducing the race- and class-based inequities structuring our district. But in the Rainbow conflict, we were representing our own beliefs and the views of our closest supporters. If the majority of our district's constituencies had effectively organized for their viewpoints and beliefs, the resulting dialogue might have been even more democratic, and the outcome might have been quite different.

In conflicts about schooling equity in which I found myself in the minority on the board, I often wished that the district's majority constituencies had effectively organized to counter school board policies that, in my view, denied equity of opportunity to students of color. The board's aborted effort to improve the selection processes of the district's gifted program, discussed in Chapter 4, is one example. Had the district's majority constituencies organized to influence that conflict, the outcome might well have been quite different. Thus Gutmann's (1987) vision of the role of participative dialogue in democratic education requires a corrective component—the incorporation of an analysis of power disparities and how they might be overcome.

Still, Gutmann's view of conscious social reproduction of the society as the ultimate purpose of democratic education differs significantly from how education's purposes are usually defined. Most definitions rarely privilege the needs of the society, as Gutmann's does. Instead, they often focus on the needs of the economy for educated and skilled participants. When education's ultimate purpose is not defined as meeting the needs of the economy, it is usually defined as serving the individual demands of parents for schooling that advances their children's futures. Gutmann's definition of the purpose of democratic education as serving the common good of conscious social reproduction is an implicit critique of much current debate about the purposes of schooling.

The current stress on choice as a panacea, for example, has led many choice proponents to concentrate on the individual and familial purposes of education and to ignore or trivialize the relationships between education and the greater good of the larger society. As an example of such reduction, consider the argument that Paul Hill (2001) makes in "What Is Public About Public Education," the culminating essay in Terry M. Moe's edited collection, *A Primer on America's Schools.*

Hill wants to propose an expansive definition of public education. He proceeds by constructing and analyzing the following scenario: A mother, Patricia, removes her daughter, Sarie, from a public school in which Sarie is not doing well, and uses a publicly funded voucher to enroll her in a religious school. Hill then poses three questions:

- Did the mother's action weaken public education?
- Was the voucher program she chose destructive of public education?
- Was the religious school she chose, as well as its supporters, harming public education?

Although I take issue with how Hill (2001) poses and answers all three questions, I am most interested in his treatment of his initial question. Hill transforms that first question—Did the mother's action (in choosing religious education and a publicly funded voucher) weaken public education?—into an examination of the value of sacrifice. Hill rephrases the question as, Should the mother sacrifice her child's future to altruistic action by keeping her in the public school?

Sacrifice, for Hill (2001), represents the idea that the mother "has an obligation to fight for others' children" (p. 295). Hill uses Albert Hirschman's categories of exit, voice, and loyalty, from Hirschman's classic 1970 text that examines issues of choice in consumer, corporate, and governmental settings, to explore the mother's options. Hill interprets Hirschman as arguing that parents "should use voice rather than exit because their demands for school quality can lead to improvements that benefit all students" (Hill, 2001, p. 295).

Hill then asserts that Hirschman is wrong, because school improvement is a zero-sum terrain in which some parents' gain will be other parents' loss. "Thus, demanding parents who stay in a troubled school might not raise its overall quality," Hill concludes. "They can corner the best it has to offer, possibly leaving the remaining students with below-average classes and teachers" (p. 296).

This is a reductive and individualist view of the results of school-change efforts. It defines parent action as producing benefits only for one's own child, rather than changing the way the school operates so that instruction improves for all students. Hill (2001) advances no evidence for this constricted definition. Nor does he support the assertion that schooling improvement or the benefits of parent change efforts are constrained by zero-sum limits. But note what Hirschman (1970) actually argued:

> Parents who plan to shift their children from public to private school may thereby contribute to a further deterioration in public education. If they realize this prospective effect of their decision they may end up not taking it, for reasons of general welfare or even as the result of a private cost-benefit calculation: the lives of both parents and children will be affected by the quality of public education in their community, and if this quality deteriorates, the higher educational attainments of the children to be obtained by

shifting them to private school have a cost which could be so large as to counsel against the shift. (pp. 100–101)

Hirschman's (1970) argument includes a consideration of the effects of parent exit on all public education and ultimately on the "general welfare" of the broader community. Hirschman's reasoning is much closer to Gutmann's (1987) notion of conscious social reproduction than to Hill's argument about the zero-sum limits of parent activism. Hill (2001) argues that "Hirschman assumed that the quality of a school's services is indivisible, so that an improvement made to satisfy a vocal parent benefits all. That turns out to be wrong, at least most of the time" (p. 297). But Hirschman argued that when parents consider a shift from public to private education, they may well balance the benefits to their child against the costs to the larger community of which they are part. They may even decide that the benefits to their child will be outweighed by the harm to the community, and ultimately to themselves as community members. To counter Hirschman, Hill would have to argue that choosing private schooling benefits, rather than harms, the entire community, a much more difficult task.

Next, consider Hill's (2001) notion that "a heroic parent's effort to turn around a low-performing school" (pp. 294–295) may at best result only in individual change for the child, possibly to the detriment of other children. But suppose the "heroic parent" does not take on the effort to improve her child's schooling as an individual crusade. In Hill's scenario, the mother has talked with other parents who express similar concerns about the school's inadequacies, and has even gone to the principal as part of a small group. Why shouldn't the heroic parent and the other parents she has identified begin to organize the school's parent body into a campaign for school improvement?

Many urban parents, no longer prepared to tolerate the failures of inner-city schools, are organizing such campaigns across the country. The recent literature on parent involvement has chronicled the shift from the individual heroic-parent effort that Hill's analysis decries, to group-based community-organizing efforts to generate and sustain school improvement campaigns (Beam, Eskenazi, & Kamber, 2002; Beam & Irani, 2003; Gold, Simon, & Brown, 2002; Lopez, 2003; Mediratta, 2004; Mediratta, Fruchter, & Lewis, 2002; Mediratta & Karp, 2003; Shirley, 1997; Talbot, 2004; Warren, 2001, 2005; Zachary & olatoye, 2001).

Moreover, national and regional community-organizing groups such as ACORN (the Association of Community Organizations for Reform Now), PICO (People Improving Communities Through Organizing), IAF (the Industrial Areas Foundation), the Gamaliel Foundation, DART (Direct

Action and Research Training Center), and others support such organizing efforts by recruiting and training organizers, as well as by providing strategic guidance, information, and support to local affiliates launching school improvement efforts.

I focus on community organizing for education reform, rather than the heroic efforts of Hill's individual parent, because such organizing provides new levers to improve failing schools in urban districts. Moreover, such organizing can begin to actualize Gutmann's (1987) notion of democratic education. Organizing offers a way to challenge, through participatory dialogue, the entrenched power that has imposed failing schools on poor neighborhoods.

Consider that if a school is failing one parent's child, it is likely to be failing many others. A school that fails to serve its students is also failing the wider community, which includes, but transcends, the school's parent body. Therefore a failing school is a community concern that community organizing should address, to improve the well-being and vitality of the community's current and future citizens.

Moreover, note that Hill (2001) has not identified the race or class dimensions of his scenario. Patricia and Sarie could be living anywhere, except that they are able to enroll in a religious school and use the voucher to help pay the tuition. But as my earlier discussions of the race-based achievement gap and the failures of audit-based accountability demonstrated, failing schools such as the one Sarie originally attended are overwhelmingly located in inner-city neighborhoods in which poor families of color have been segregated. Changing the dynamics of failing schools in such situations is only possible through collective efforts, rather than by the heroic individual acts of futile sacrifice that Hill posits.

Hill (2001) presents Patricia's choice to remove her daughter, Sarie, from the failing school as the only viable parent choice, and he defends Patricia from charges of failing her moral obligations. But taking collective action to improve the quality of a failing school is hardly a moral obligation. Increasingly, in inner-city settings where failing schools have been tolerated by political elites for decades, it can be a quite practical step to take.

Hill (2001) concludes his discussion of whether the parent's choice of private education weakens public education by rephrasing the original question. It now becomes: "Do the parents of children who are not well served by their neighborhood schools have an obligation as citizens to stand and fight?" Consider Hill's answer:

> Surely no. Individuals should not have to sacrifice their own children's future for a vague possibility of helping others and are certainly not compelled to engage in a fruitless effort. In a situation where a parent has no assurance

that her actions can improve schooling for other children, her private interest and the goals of public education point in the same direction. Patricia [the mother in the scenario] should do anything she can to make sure her child learns the skills and habits necessary for full membership in adult society. (p. 297)

This is the counsel of radical individualism, shorn of connection to, let alone concern with, the welfare of the larger community. Hill argues that a parent should not feel obligated to act for more than private, familial goals unless she is assured that her actions will be successful. This principle precludes all collective action for any broader purpose; how can anyone be assured that their actions will prove successful before they act? Such assurance is hard to come by in the real world.

Hill (2001) has structured his scenario so that any action except the exercise of individual choice of exit is excluded from possibility. Although he accepts that education is a public as well as a private good whose public dimensions can have "real impact on the community as a whole" (p. 297), his discussion radically simplifies the available options, divorces choice from broader community concerns, and focuses choice solely on private and familial dimensions. His reduction of parent action to individual choice of exit removes the possibility of collective action, through organizing, from the realm of possible responses. But education organizing for school reform is rapidly becoming an actionable response to failing schools in urban settings across the country.

EDUCATION ORGANIZING IN URBAN SETTINGS

Community organizing for school improvement can challenge and disrupt the power hierarchies that traditionally dominate urban areas. Counter to Hill's reductionism, such organizing represents an opportunity to transform failing schools in many inner-city neighborhoods. In 2002 the Cross-City Campaign for Urban School Reform and Research for Action published a study that included a national scan of education organizing. The study identified more than 200 groups engaged in specific organizing efforts (Gold et al., 2002). In the same year, the New York University Institute for Education and Social Policy's Community Involvement Program conducted a study of community organizing for school reform and found almost 100 groups working to improve public schooling in only eight sites across the country (Mediratta et al., 2002).

Dennis Shirley, Mark Warren, Eva Gold and Elaine Simon, Charles Payne, John Beam, Marion Orr, and my colleague Kavitha Mediratta have analyzed the school reform efforts of adult and youth groups across the country. Their work has documented a burgeoning movement that is mobilizing communities to transform the power relations that impose failing schools on poor children of color, to achieve the kind of public accountability that middle-class communities have exercised for decades.

Organizing is the direct action of communities that are disenfranchised by the traditional exercise of American economic and political power. That direct action results from countless hours of individual engagement, discussion, relationship building, trust development, strategic planning, and campaign mobilization. Those processes develop public demonstrations of community power, designed to persuade authorities to respond. As one organizer who was quoted in Mediratta's (2004) study defined the work:

> "The job of the organizer and of the core leadership is to go out into that neighborhood and organize tenant associations, block associations, and neighborhood campaigns. To go out and knock on people's doors and say, 'What are your concerns? Do other people have the same problems? Are you interested in starting a tenants' association to build some power to fix the problem?' We help people understand that as individuals they don't have power. There's not much they can do, the landlord won't listen to them, and the city probably won't listen to them. But as a group, they do. The group can pressure the landlord, or the city, or the bank to fix their building. We're teaching them the power of collective action through tenant organizing." (p. 21)[1]

VARIATION IN EDUCATION ORGANIZING

Different organizing groups employ different methods. Some target disenfranchised neighborhoods and send organizers on door-to-door campaigns to recruit potential members and identify the issues that neighborhood residents seek to resolve. Others build coalitions of institutional members such as religious congregations, neighborhood organizations, schools, and unions. The coalition members then determine the issues that organizing campaigns will address.

Many organizations conduct what they call relational organizing, by working with school, district, and even state-level authorities. Mark Warren (2005), in a comprehensive article in the *Harvard Educational Review*, distinguishes relational organizing from a more traditional strategy that he defines as unilateral power organizing. Unilateral power strategies, in Warren's view, organize "the social capital of their community to leverage power into the political arena to force public, and sometimes private, institutions to improve services or to provide funds to build affordable housing or support economic development" (p. 138). Groups using relational organizing strategies "are willing to confront powerful institutions, but only when recalcitrant elites refuse to negotiate. They approach schools as partners, but this does not mean ignoring tensions and conflicts" (p. 138).

WHAT EDUCATION ORGANIZING CAN ACCOMPLISH

Although the approaches may differ, the goal of unilateral and relational organizing is to build powerful organizations that can resolve issues and win victories that improve living conditions for their membership and the broader community. Austin Interfaith, for example, a local affiliate of the state-level Texas Interfaith Education Foundation (TIEF) of the national Industrial Areas Foundation, works to make instruction more effective by transforming school cultures through teacher-parent-community collaboration. But the schools Austin Interfaith organizes are affiliated with more than 100 Alliance Schools established through collaboration between the TIEF and the Texas State Education Department. Funding for Alliance Schools' after-school programs and other supplementary supports is provided by an annual appropriation of the Texas legislature, an appropriation ensured by the power of the TIEF.

The Oakland Community Organization (OCO), a coalition of religious congregations and community groups that includes schools as members, launched a campaign more than a decade ago to improve achievement outcomes for Oakland's poor students of color by starting small schools in Oakland's flatlands. OCO, an affiliate of the national People Improving Communities through Organizing, or PICO, worked with the Oakland school system to develop the new schools on a base of shared governance, to ensure that the new school cultures were responsive to student, parent, and community needs. When the Oakland school system was taken over by the state for fiscal mismanagement, OCO's affiliates across the state used PICO's clout in the California legislature to ensure that Oakland's small-schools experiment would continue.

Congregational leaders in Miami PACT (People Acting for Community Together), a local affiliate of DART (Direct Action and Research Training Center), were concerned about the low reading levels in many of Miami-Dade's schools serving African American and Latino students. PACT's education committee, congregation members who were primarily retired teachers and administrators, decided that the district's reading curriculum needing strengthening. After much investigation, the committee recommended that the district implement Direct Instruction, a heavily phonics-based and scripted reading program, in a sample of the district's most poorly performing elementary schools.

Faced with initial resistance from school district administrators, PACT mounted a campaign that mobilized thousands of members to demand the introduction of Direct Instruction. The district eventually acceded and implemented the program, first on a pilot basis and eventually in almost 30 district schools. PACT members organized local school committees to monitor program implementation.[2]

The transformation of teacher leadership in New York City's Community School District 9 provides another example. The Community Collaboration to Improve District 9 Schools (CC9) in South Bronx neighborhoods evolved from a local organizing group's inability to get the school district to improve its poorly performing schools. This neighborhood group then led an effort to develop a strong coalition of community groups committed to school improvement. Each group recruited local parents into a districtwide coalition that developed an improvement platform and launched a districtwide campaign to implement it. The resulting coalition, CC9,[3] identified improvements in teacher quality, school leadership, and school-community relationships as its target priorities, and decided to concentrate its initial efforts on improving teacher quality.

After intensive research, CC9 defined a reform effort called the Lead Teacher program. Lead Teachers would be master teachers from across the city system, recruited into poorly performing schools in District 9 through a $10,000 annual (and pensionable) salary increment. The Lead Teachers would teach half time and coach, mentor, train, and support beginning teachers in their nonteaching time.

CC9 organized a districtwide campaign, with strong teacher union support, to persuade the city school system to implement the Lead Teacher program. The New York City schools chancellor eventually agreed to implement the program, and provided almost $2 million in city funds to support it. Thirty-six Lead Teachers began work in 10 poorly performing district schools in the 2004–5 school year. During that initial year, attrition among the cohort of teachers supported by the Lead Teachers was reduced from 28% to 16% in the target schools (*First Year Evaluation*, 2005).[4] The latest contract negotiated by the city and the teachers' union includes an expansion of the Lead Teacher program to the school system's low-performing schools.

The work of Chicago ACORN provides yet another example. For more than 2 decades, Chicago ACORN has organized parent groups in three west side African American and Latino neighborhoods. Faced with persistently poor achievement outcomes in those neighborhoods' schools, ACORN members began to investigate issues of teacher quality. They discovered that their local schools had high numbers of inexperienced teachers and very high rates of teacher attrition. Worse, the school system's teacher recruitment efforts were unable to fully staff neighborhood schools by the start of each school year.

Chicago ACORN produced a report that demonstrated the severity of the recruitment and attrition issues in its target neighborhoods. But ACORN kept the Chicago school system informed of its efforts and shared the report with system administrators before publication. What resulted was an agreement between ACORN and the school system to improve recruitment and to investigate how to resolve the core issue of high teacher attrition.

Working with Logan Square Neighborhood Association (LSNA), a sophisticated local organizing group, ACORN decided that LSNA's efforts to recruit and train parent activists to become teachers could be generalized into a citywide program. ACORN and LSNA then built a coalition to develop and implement the Grow Your Own (GYO) teacher recruitment and training program, in conjunction with Chicago's teacher-training institutions, to prepare neighborhood parents to become teachers in their local schools. The coalition, led by ACORN, convinced the state legislature and the Illinois governor to approve and fund the program with an initial allocation of $1.5 million, to be increased to $10 million over the following 5 years. The first cohort of GYO parents are currently enrolled in programs at Chicago colleges.

As a final example, consider the work of South Central Youth Empowered Through Action (SCYEA), the youth group of Los Angeles' Community Coalition for Substance Abuse Prevention and Treatment. SCYEA has been organizing for several years to improve college access for poor students of color in the Los Angeles Unified School District (LAUSD). After leading and winning a campaign to expand student access to guidance counselors, SCYEA began organizing to expand California's A-G college-bound curriculum, previously limited to top-track students, to all LAUSD's high school students. In the summer of 2005, the Los Angeles district agreed to offer its A-G curriculum to all high school students and to provide the academic supports students need to successfully negotiate that curriculum.

These vignettes illustrate what community groups can achieve through organizing for school reform. Each group recruited its membership, established its particular organizational structure, identified its core issues, developed its strategies, enlisted critical allies, and organized its campaigns somewhat differently. But all the groups organized local constituencies to transform the traditional power relationships limiting the effectiveness of public education in their communities. They leveraged the power of their local groups to persuade school system leadership, through combinations of relational and unilateral power organizing, to implement the schooling improvements the groups sought. These organizing practices represent a powerful alternative to the dichotomy of exiting public education or making an individually heroic but futile sacrifice of one's child that Hill's chapter posed.

THE CONTEXT OF EDUCATION ORGANIZING

Community organizing has developed in cycles across the past century. A surge of such organizing in the 1930s was supported by several of the member unions of the Congress of Industrial Organizations (CIO). Housing and tenant organizing, sharecropper organizing, welfare-recipient organizing, and student and farmworker organizing complemented the mass movements of the 1960s and 1970s. The current wave of education organizing emerged in the late 1980s in many urban settings and is being driven by an interrelated set of conditions:

- The economic and political marginalization of poor inner-city communities of color, enforced by segregation, middle-class flight, the departure of industry, and the refusal of urban elites to invest in and support the improvement of city schools in poor neighborhoods
- Recurrent cycles of fiscal crises, primarily caused by eroding urban tax bases, which significantly reduce the funding available to sustain, let alone improve, schooling in poor inner-city neighborhoods
- Increasingly persuasive linkages between educational attainment and economic success in a postindustrial, knowledge-based economy, which has convinced many inner-city parents of the necessity to secure more effective education for their children
- Imposition of state and federal performance-based accountability systems, which has forced many urban school districts to release and disseminate the school-level outcomes of city and state testing and to disaggregate those outcomes by race, gender, language use, and special education status

Because these conditions show little sign of receding, we may be on the crest of a national expansion of education organizing. If such an increase is likely, what are the implications of these organizing efforts to improve student educational achievement, and school-level educational outcomes, in many of the nation's most poorly performing urban schools and districts? If changing the dynamics of school failure is possible through collective organizing efforts, rather than through the futile sacrifice that Hill's scenario posits, what are these collective efforts achieving?

ASSESSING THE RESULTS OF EDUCATION ORGANIZING

The most immediate implications concern student and school outcomes: Do these organizing efforts lead to improvements in schools that result in higher student achievement? The question is complicated because the results of education organizing are necessarily indirect. When education succeeds, it produces increases in student knowledge, skills, and capacity. Because education is a deeply collaborative undertaking, teachers and administrators coproduce these outcomes with students, in schools. Yet organizers work outside schools, in surrounding neighborhoods, and primarily with parents and community members, except for those growing numbers of groups that directly organize youth. Therefore education organizing must work from the outside to improve the instructional practices, the culture of relationships, and the overarching climate of schools that produce student knowledge and youth development.

Thus answering the question of whether organizing for schooling improvement produces gains in student achievement requires complex research efforts. Such research must identify the strategies that organizing groups launch to improve what goes on inside schools. Research must then assess the effectiveness of these organizing strategies in transforming the particular components of schools' instructional core, professional culture, or climate that each group's efforts target. Then research must link improvements in those components to the results in terms of schooling change and, ultimately, to improvements in student achievement.

This research involves even more complexity because education organizing occurs within schools in which other reform efforts are constantly being introduced. Many schools, especially in urban areas, are implementing new reading and math curricula, new professional development regimens, and new measures of classroom management and student discipline. To isolate the effects of organizing, research must find ways to control for all the other school-level reform and improvement efforts that are simultaneously under way.

Such efforts are difficult but not impossible to implement. For the past 4 years, the New York University Institute for Education and Social Policy's Community Involvement Program (CIP) has been conducting a research project, funded by the Charles Stewart Mott Foundation, to determine how community organizing affects student achievement outcomes. This research tracks the work of many of the groups described above, examines their influence on district policy and local school conditions, and analyzes how their efforts contribute to improvements in the quality of education, and the resulting student outcomes, in their neighborhood schools. CIP's researchers define their task as follows:

> To analyze improvements in the core capacities of schools targeted by each study group, we will develop indicators that reflect each group's specific campaign goals, as well as a wide variety of intermediary changes in schools that can be assessed with available data. These intermediary variables can include, for example, measures of change in the school's professional culture, using indicators such as teacher attendance, teacher retention, teacher experience, teacher certification, leadership stability, facility utilization rates, student-teacher ratios, suspension rates or discipline referrals in a school. Our analysis will examine changes in these indicators over time, in the schools targeted by the group compared to the school district as a whole, and where possible and relevant, to a group of similar schools in the same district. Where there is sufficient evidence of gains in schooling capacity, as demonstrated by positive changes in intermediary indicators, we will define, and examine the change in, a broad set of outcome indicators of improvement in schools, compared to school systems as a whole. (quoted in Mediratta, 2004, p. 45)

CIP's study is designed to demonstrate the relationships between community-organizing efforts to improve schools and districts and the resulting effects of that organizing on student achievement. But the study will explore other dimensions of organizing as well. Mark Warren (2005), for example, analyzes social capital as a capacity of both schools and neighborhoods and hypothesizes that it will increase as schools and neighborhoods collaborate through forms of relational organizing. He argues that such collaborative efforts to advance school reform can increase the social capital of both schools and communities. Other research on community organizing for school reform has begun to illumine how, and in what ways, such organizing not only enhances community social capital, but also increases neighborhood-based accountability and democratic participation. CIP's research will explore the following two linkages.

EDUCATION ORGANIZING CAN INCREASE
NEIGHBORHOOD SOCIAL CAPITAL

Theorists such as Pierre Bourdieu (1970), James Coleman (1988), and Robert Putnam (1995) have defined social capital as the level of trust between members of a given community. Increasing trust between neighborhood members generates a variety of social gains: More trusting relationships increase neighborhood solidarity, help build varieties of networks across neighborhood residents, and strengthen the potential for launching collective action to meet neighborhood needs. Mark Schneider, Paul Teske, and Melissa Marschall (2000) provide an interesting effort to measure the differential development of social capital in their book *Choosing Schools: Consumer Choice and the Quality of American Schools.*

To assess the effects of public school choice, Schneider et al. develop comparisons between two New York City school districts, one offering a wide range of choice and the other offering little choice, as well as two New Jersey suburban districts offering the same contrasts.

In one of their analyses, they assess whether school choice can affect neighborhood stocks of social capital. Using survey responses collected from parents in all four districts, they define PTA membership, the extent of parent volunteerism in schools, the number of contacts with other parents about schooling issues, and the level of trust parents have in their children's teachers as variables measuring social capital. Their analysis finds that for all four variables, parents in choice districts register higher levels than do nonchoice parents:

> Our research shows that in both an urban and suburban setting and under different institutional settings of choice, the act of school choice seems to stimulate parents to become more involved in a wide range of school-related activities that build social capital. (p. 237)

Set aside whether PTA membership, volunteerism, parent contacts, and parent trust in teachers are useful measures of community social capital. And set aside the question of how school choice stimulates parents to become more broadly involved in Schneider et al.'s measures of social capital, because their analysis doesn't specify the intervening mechanisms. But if increasing public school choice can somehow contribute to increasing levels of social capital, organizing efforts to improve public education can make even more powerful contributions. The relationships that organizing builds are far more direct, intensive, and collective than the effects of choice.

Consider the specific ways in which organizing can contribute to enhancing neighborhood social capital. The individual engagement that organizing groups employ, through one-on-one interactions, build a primary basis of what Bryk and Schneider (2002) define as relational trust. Group meetings, issue deliberations, and strategy sessions can intensify those bonds of individual trust by expanding them to wider forums. The large-scale actions that organizing groups mount, as well as the periodic conferences, conventions, and conclaves they stage, can further expand those bonds into affirmations of group solidarity. These expanding levels of trust can extend the capacity of community members to act collectively to improve the quality of public education that their children receive. Building these levels of relational trust, and increasing neighborhood capacity for collective activity, can contribute to increasing the levels of social capital in the neighborhoods in which organizing groups work. CIP's research into the effects of education organizing is attempting to assess whether neighborhood social capital increases as a result of such organizing.

Several theorists, including Coleman (1988) and Putnam (1995), have linked higher levels of social capital to increasing the capacity for democratic participation, at neighborhood, city, and even regional levels. If education organizing can increase neighborhood levels of social capital, such organizing can also contribute to expanded capacity for democratic participation in formerly disenfranchised and politically marginalized neighborhoods.

EDUCATION ORGANIZING CAN INCREASE ACCOUNTABILITY AND EXPAND CAPACITY FOR DEMOCRATIC PARTICIPATION

CIP's research demonstrates that organizers and leaders work to build resident capacity to exercise accountability in poor neighborhoods of color that have been denied participation in schooling governance (Mediratta, 2004; Mediratta & Karp, 2003; Mediratta et al., 2002; Zachary and olatoye, 2001). In most urban school districts, opportunities for citizen participation are quite limited, whether urban school boards have been elected or appointed. Parents and community members in poor neighborhoods have historically had very limited opportunities to participate in critical schooling decisions or exercise any accountability over their individual schools. The recent concentration of education power in mayoral hierarchies is simply the latest manifestation of the centralized control of urban school systems.

Education organizing can provide venues for neighborhood parents to challenge these top-down forms of control over schooling. Through local community-organizing campaigns, parents can make demands on their school systems, monitor school and system performance, and take action when that performance is inadequate. To effectively exercise such bottom-up accountability, organizing groups educate and train their members about how schools and school systems function and how they can operate more effectively. Through such training, members become familiar with schooling issues such as effective instruction and meaningful professional development. They learn about the differing benefits of small class size and a longer school day, or consider whether student support is best provided by guidance counselors or advisories. Most important, members learn how to obtain and assess schooling data, primarily indicators of student achievement, to decide how effectively the school and the district are educating their children.

This accumulation of member knowledge and understanding about how schools and districts work, and how their performance might be improved, is critical to organizing groups' capacity to hold educators accountable for school and system performance. When increased member knowledge and understanding is linked to the capacity to act, strategically and powerfully, to persuade schools and districts to improve, what can result is bottom-up accountability—the ability to hold local schools and systems responsible for student and school-level academic outcomes. Thus new forms of accountability can emerge from education organizing at the neighborhood level. Participating in these new forms of accountability can enhance the capacity for democratic participation in poor communities. Moreover, this increased community capacity to demand accountability in education can help organizing groups make similar demands on other public and private services. Ultimately, increasing community capacity for accountability can contribute to increasing the capacity for the kind of democratic education that Gutmann (1987) espouses. In communities in which such organizing is occurring, these efforts have begun to reduce the power differentials that prevent genuine democratic dialogue about conscious social reproduction.

Most education organizing groups do not set out to build neighborhood social capacity and enhance local potential for increased democratic participation. But through the exercise of unilateral or relational power, effective education organizing groups can contribute to the development of neighborhood social capital. That increased social capital can contribute to the capacity for democratic participation in our most distressed and disenfranchised urban communities.

The ossified power of traditional urban elites, the limited capacity of urban districts, and the failure of the public will of urban residents to demand improvement of schools serving poor children of color creates a power deadlock that has imposed poor schooling on poor communities of color for generations. Organizing efforts can intervene to break such power deadlocks because organizing mobilizes new forms of community power.

In the initial chapters of this book I argue, for example, that to reduce the black-white achievement gap in the nation's urban education systems, the culture of schooling must be transformed. But as demonstrated by the example of the Pittsburgh school system's response to the student strike that Robby Wideman helped to initiate, schooling authorities—whether superintendents; school boards; or more recently, mayors—are often incapable of understanding why schooling cultures need to change. When organizing mobilizes sufficient constituency power, it can intervene to expose, and transform, the power relationships that resist such understanding.

In Chapter 3, I argue that accountability systems based on audit principles can measure school and systems outcomes, but cannot provide the supports necessary to define and implement the necessary improvement strategies. Organizing can initiate processes of inspection at the school level, identify critical schooling problems and capacity needs, and define the specific interventions and supports necessary to help schools improve.

Chapter 4 demonstrates why choice is no panacea for improving urban schools; there, I argue that not only choice schools, but all schools, need support from external sources such as districts. Organizing can force districts that have tolerated poorly performing schools for decades to provide those schools with the supports they need to improve their student outcomes.

In the preceding chapter I argued for the necessity of direct district action for reform and provided three examples of how comprehensive district reform significantly improved student achievement and reduced race-based achievement gaps. Those districts launched their reforms without the spur of organizing campaigns. But organizing can force districts too callous or recalcitrant to initiate reform to launch improvement efforts, as the example of the Lead Teacher campaign waged by CC9 demonstrates. Before the CC9 organizing groups initiated their campaign to improve the quality of teaching, District 9 contained several of the city's most poorly performing schools. Under the direction of a new regional superintendent, and with the spur of CC9 and the Lead Teacher program, District 9 schools made the highest test score gains of all New York City's school districts in the 2004–5 school year.[5]

Just as choice is not a panacea, so community organizing for school reform is not a silver bullet that can resolve the schooling failures caused by decades of district neglect. Nor can community organizing necessarily force a redirection of public will among citizenries that have tolerated failing schools in poor communities of color for decades. As Peter Dreier (2005) observes:

> All community organizing groups, even the most effective, mobilize a relatively small number of people. Unlike most labor union campaigns . . . community organizing only requires that there are enough people mobilized to disrupt business as usual, to get an issue into the media, or to catalyze allies

who have influence over public officials or corporate leaders. Most successful community organizing involves using a group's very limited resources in strategic ways. (p. 8)

What community organizing at the local level can accomplish is to disrupt the power stasis that has prevented poor schooling for students of color from becoming an issue that urban public will must confront. Hopefully what will follow the current expansion of community organizing for school reform is protracted struggle, in urban areas across the country, about how to improve schools that have been allowed to fail students of color for decades. And hopefully, in response to those struggles, we will find the public will to do what we have never before accomplished in this nation—provide poor students of color with the high-quality education they have the right to receive.

Notes

INTRODUCTION

1. Proponents of market-based solutions often cite research-based findings about the superior performance of choice initiatives, such as vouchers, as well as the comparative effectiveness of private schools; Catholic schools; and more recently, charter schools, as evidence of public school failure. But as research methodologies become increasingly sophisticated, newer studies are beginning to revise the research evidence of public school ineffectiveness. Recent studies based on data from the National Assessment of Educational Progress (NAEP), carried out by the National Center for Education Statistics (2005) under the George W. Bush administration, have demonstrated that charter school achievement lags behind public school achievement. See *The Charter School Dust-Up*, by Carnoy, Jacobsen, Mishel, and Rothstein (2005), for an analysis of recent research evidence that establishes the limited outcomes of charter schools. New studies exploring private school/public school outcomes are demonstrating that when advanced methodologies are employed to control for student background differences, the vaunted private and Catholic school performance superiority vanishes. See, for example, *Charter, Private, Public Schools and Academic Achievement: New Evidence from NAEP Mathematics Data*, by Lubienski and Lubienski (2006). As scholarship advances, the results of more studies will continue to challenge the claims that public education is inferior to private school education, Catholic school education, charter school education, or voucher-provided education. What remains to be seen is whether the myth of universal public school failure will be similarly deconstructed.

CHAPTER 1

1. The latest census data is even more dramatic. In 2000, approximately 30% of U.S. students went to public schools in metropolitan areas, 43% attended public schools in suburbs or large towns, and 27% attended public schools in small towns or rural areas (National Center for Education Statistics, 2006).

CHAPTER 2

1. See also Baldwin (1979). Remember George Bernard Shaw's aphorism, "A language is a dialect with an army."

2. In her discussion of the centrality of culture, Ladson-Billings (1994) observes that too many monocultural Americans think of culture as an attribute of exotic others, assuming that "culture is what other people have; what we have is just truth" (p. 131).

CHAPTER 3

1. Dr. Rudy Crew, the New York City school chancellor during much of the 5 years of the New York Networks for School Renewal project, did not support the project's conception of a Learning Zone. But Crew's opposition was not solely determinative. The networks of schools that were conceived as the building blocks of the Learning Zone never cohered.

2. In some states, particularly in the Deep South, Title I expenditures have represented almost 20% of total public education spending.

3. Vermont was for some time reportedly considering this trade-off, since the Vermont state education agency supposedly calculated that the cost of implementing the NCLB requirements would considerably exceed what the state is allocated in federal Title I funds.

4. Opportunity-to-learn standards were originally included in the set of standards promulgated as part of the Goals 2000 initiative. As a result of a long congressional fight, opportunity-to-learn standards were omitted from the set of national standards advocated by the administration of President Bill Clinton and such national reform groups as Achieve, the National Governors Association, and the Education Commission of the States.

CHAPTER 4

1. Given approximately 600 students in the gifted program, the meeting's audience was approximately 25% of the total possible audience if every program student's parents had attended.

2. Beatrice S. Fennimore (2005) provides two similar narratives of how districts use gifted programs to frustrate the mandate of *Brown*.

3. Most media accounts failed to mention that for decades, New Orleans had one of the nation's worst-performing public school systems.

4. It is possible that the failure to mobilize for choice is a generational phenomenon in African American communities. Fuller argues, "My generation pushed for social change through government solutions, but younger blacks are much more interested in private initiatives. They understand that the public school

system cannot by itself be the solution to educating low-income children" (Tierney, 2006).

5. The East Harlem neighborhood is currently facing gentrification as real estate values continue to skyrocket throughout much of New York City.

6. But see Chapter 5: "What School Choice Really Means: Fact and PR in East Harlem," in Kirp (2002), for some indication of how the selection process operated in District Four, as well as a similar view of the hierarchy that resulted.

7. This point is made by Kirp.

8. Schneider et al. (2000) convincingly demonstrate why this claim greatly exaggerates the potentials of choice.

9. As a school board member in District 15 when Alvarado began to develop schools of choice in District 2, I can testify to the drain of successful teachers out of our district as they were recruited to start and staff new schools in District 2.

10. Schneider et al. (2000) attempt to control for teacher quality in their analysis of the district's test score performance across time. But the indicator they use for teacher quality, percentage of teachers with more than 5 years' experience, does not adequately capture the characteristics of the creative teachers choice schools sought. My Brooklyn district, for example, aggressively recruited graduates of Bank Street College of Education's master's program to staff our gifted program classrooms and choice schools. Many of the teachers District 4 recruited had less than 5 years' experience, but had already demonstrated the creative attributes the district sought to staff its choice schools.

11. Much charter school research has demonstrated the toll of the additional burdens schools endure when they must design and carry out these operational functions themselves (Ascher et al., 2000, 2003).

CHAPTER 5

1. In July 2003, as a result of a citywide educational reorganization as one of the consequences of mayoral control of education, District 2 ceased to exist as an educational subdistrict and was subsumed within the city's new regional education structure.

2. In an Education Policy Analysis Archives exchange, Lois Weiner, professor of elementary and secondary education at New Jersey City University, challenges the accuracy of the research that establishes the scale of achievement results in District 2, and Lauren Resnick, the director of Pittsburgh University's Learning Research and Development Center, defends it (Weiner, 2003; Resnick, 2003). Weiner argues that District 2 was and is a quite segregated district, that achievement outcomes continue to correlate with the extent of segregation, and that the instructional reforms were imposed on a resistant teacher population. Our institute's analyses validate Weiner's argument that the reforms did not change the patterns of district segregation. But our analyses also suggest that many of the district's schools' results, including the most segregated, improved significantly. Moreover, the percentage of students in the district's elementary schools reading

below the 50th percentile decreased from 47% to 35% across the decade of Alvarado's superintendency. The decline in the percentage of middle school students reading below the 50th percentile was even more dramatic.

3. The Kauffman Foundation subsequently provided funding for a comprehensive evaluation of FTF, which was conducted by a team from Youth Development Strategies (YDSI). When the U.S. Department of Education's Institute for Educational Sciences funded the FTF scale-up initiative, MDRC was engaged to produce an evaluation of the initiative. My summary of FTF's work in Kansas City, Kansas, is based on the accounts in *Turning the Tide* (Gambone et al., 2004) and *The Challenge of Scaling Up Educational Reform* (Quint et al., 2005), as well as IRRE's final report to the Institute for Education Sciences, *First Things First: From Getting Off the Dime to Getting It on the Ground* (Connell, 2005).

4. The YDSI evaluation defined the walkthroughs as an accountability tool "because they helped district administrators to better understand how, and whether, classrooms were engaging environments . . . they signaled to teachers that engagement was a district priority" (Gambone et al., 2004, p. 67). Walkthroughs in District 2 played a similar role, though they were more focused on assessing the effectiveness of the principal planning and professional development strategies launched to improve instruction.

5. Note that although these are impressive gains, and although the trend lines are all on strong upward curves, the Kansas City, Kansas, district is still scoring below optimal levels of student achievement.

6. The two evaluations used differing methodologies. MDRC's evaluation employed a comparative interrupted time-series analysis. YDSI's evaluation used a probability optimal/risk-level analysis with baselines as comparisons.

7. Through Tennessee law, residents of the state's four largest cities—Memphis, Nashville, Knoxville, and Chattanooga—can form and dissolve their urban school systems by vote. Chattanooga voted to constitute its city system in 1941. In 1996, frustrated at the need to pay both county and city taxes to maintain its school system, and disillusioned at the inability of Chattanooga schools to improve students' outcomes, a majority of Chattanooga's voters dissolved the city system, thus forcing a merger with the county system.

8. The University of Tennessee–Chattanooga's campus abuts Chattanooga's downtown.

9. The offices of the SNS initiative were located at PEF, and two SNS codirectors, a school system appointee, and a PEF appointee, oversaw the effort. The Carnegie Corporation's program design required that a lead partner organization independent of the school system be the grant recipient and fiscal agent.

10. Register also structured a Critical Leadership Group consisting of the director of high schools, the director of the SNS initiative, Challener from the PEF, a key consultant who had been a district high school principal, Register's deputy superintendent for secondary schools, and Register himself. This group meets frequently to discuss and resolve key district issues.

11. District 2 no longer exists as a decentralized administrative unit; in 2003 it was subsumed into a larger regional structure as part of a systemic reorganiza-

tion. But teachers and administrators trained in District 2's strategies occupy key administrative and policy positions across the reorganized school system. The system's deputy chancellor for instruction from 2003 to 2006, for example, was a very effective District 2 principal.

12. A prominent effort to support comprehensive district-driven reform has been mounted by the Annenberg Institute for School Reform (AISR). AISR formed a National Task Force on Urban Districts, which produced School Communities that Work, a report and an ongoing effort to help school districts create systems of schools that achieve high standards of achievement for all students. School Communities that Work (SCtW) has developed a sophisticated set of programs, inventories, and other tools to help districts assess, enhance, and support their capacity to carry out their essential functions. SCtW's Central Office Review for Results and Equity (CORRE), for example, has helped to generate districtwide restructuring and improvement efforts in Hamilton County; Sacramento, California; Portland, Oregon; and several smaller New England urban districts. See *Framework for Action* (n.d.).

CHAPTER 6

1. My discussion of organizing owes a great debt to Mediratta's work in *Constituents of Change* (2004) and other institute publications.

2. After Dr. Rudy Crew became superintendent of the Miami-Dade school district in 2004, his suspension of the use of Direct Instruction generated a stand-off with PACT.

3. Because it has significantly expanded its scale and scope of operations, CC9 recently changed its name to CCB, the Community Collaborative to Improve Bronx Schools.

4. The data come from 7 of the 10 schools. In those schools, the average annual attrition rate was 28%, but was only 16% for the 82 teachers directly supported by the Lead Teachers.

5. Although the reorganization of the city school system under Mayor Michael Bloomberg and Chancellor Joel Klein abolished decentralized governance and the community school boards, the community school districts as geographic entities were maintained. Thus test scores and other data are still reported by community school district.

References

Ascher, C., Cole, C., Echazarreta, J., Jacobowitz, R., & McBride, Y. (2004). *Private partners and the evolution of learning communities in charter schools.* New York: New York University, Institute for Education and Social Policy.

Ascher, C., Echazarreta, J., Jacobowitz, R., McBride, Y., Troy, T., & Wamba, N. (2001). *Going charter: New models of support.* New York: New York University, Institute for Education and Social Policy.

Ascher, C., Echazarreta, J., Jacobowitz, R., McBride, Y., & Troy, T. (2003). *Governance and administrative infrastructure in New York City charter schools.* New York: New York University, Institute for Education and Social Policy.

Ascher, C., Fruchter, N., & Ikeda, K. (1998). *Schools on notice: Analysis of Schools Under Registration Review (SURR).* New York: New York University, Institute for Education and Social Policy.

Ascher, C., Fruchter, N., & Ikeda, K. (1999). *Schools in context: Final report to the New York State Education Department, 1997–1998, an analysis of SURR schools and their districts.* New York: New York University, Institute for Education and Social Policy.

Ascher, C., Jacobowitz, R., McBride, Y., & Wamba, N. (2000). *Going charter: Reflections from New York City's charter schools.* New York: New York University, Institute for Education and Social Policy.

Baldwin, J. (1979). If black English isn't a language, tell me, what is? In J. Baldwin, *The price of the ticket* (pp. 689–692). New York: St. Martin's Press.

Balkin, J. (Ed.). (2001). *What* Brown v Board *should have said.* New York: New York University Press.

Beam, J., Eskenazi, M., & Kamber, T. (2002). *Unlocking the schoolhouse door: The community struggle for a say in our children's education.* New York: Fordham University, National Center for Schools and Communities.

Beam, J., & Irani, S. (2003). *ACORN education reform organizing: Evolution of a model.* New York: National Center for Schools and Communities at Fordham University.

Bell, D. (1987). *And we are not saved: The elusive quest for racial justice.* New York: Basic Books.

Bodilly, S. (2001). *Lessons from New American Schools' scale-up phase: Prospects for bringing designs to multiple schools.* Santa Monica, CA: RAND Corporation.

Bourdieu, P. (1970). Cultural reproduction and social reproduction. Paper presented at British Sociological Conference.

Bourdieu, P., & Passeron, J. (1997). *Reproduction in education, society and culture.* Beverly Hills, CA: Sage.

Bryk, A., & Schneider, B. (2002). *Trust in schools: A core resource for improvement.* New York: Russell Sage Foundation.

Campaign for Fiscal Equity v. State of New York, 295 A.D.2d 1, 744 N.Y.S.2d 130, 2002 N.Y. App. Div. (N.Y. App. Div. 1st Dep't, 2002), modified.

Carnoy, M., Jacobsen, R., Mishel, M., & Rothstein, R. (2005). *The charter school dust-up.* Washington, DC: Economic Policy Institute; New York: Teachers College Press.

Carter, P. L. (2005). *Keepin' it real: School success beyond black and white.* New York: Oxford University Press.

Center on Education Policy. (2005). *From the capital to the classroom: Year 3 of the No Child Left Behind Act.* Washington, DC: Author.

Challener, D. (2004). What can you be when you are no longer the Dynamo of Dixie? In I. Bond & J. Ayers (Eds.), *Profiles of leadership: Innovative approaches to transforming the American high school* (pp. 73–79). Washington, DC: Alliance for Excellent Education.

Children of the Rainbow, first grade. (1991). New York City: Board of Education of the City of New York.

Chubb, J., & Moe, T. (1990). *Politics, markets, and America's schools.* Washington, DC: Brookings Institution.

Coleman, J. S. (1966). *Equality of educational opportunity.* Washington, DC: U.S. Government Printing Office.

Coleman, J. S. (1988). Social capital and the creation of human capita. *American Journal of Sociology, 94,* S95–S121.

Conchas, G. (2006). *The color of success: Race and high-achieving urban youth.* New York: Teachers College Press.

Connell, J. (2005). *First Things First: From getting off the dime to getting it on the ground.* Kansas City, KS: Institute for Research and Reform in Education.

Cook, T., Habib, F., Phillips, M., Settersten, R. A., Shagle, S. C., & Degirmencioglu, S. M. (1999). *Comer's School Development Program in Prince George's County, Maryland: A theory-based evaluation.* Evanston, IL: Northwestern University, Institute for Policy Research.

Corcoran, T., Hoppe, M., Luhm, T., & Supovitz, J. (2000). *America's Choice comprehensive school reform design: First year implementation evaluation study.* Philadelphia: Consortium for Policy Research in Education.

Damerell, R. (1968). *Triumph in a white suburb: The dramatic story of Teaneck, NJ, the first town in the nation to vote for integrated schools.* New York: W. Morrow.

Darder, A., & Torres, R. D. (2004). *After race: Racism after multiculturalism.* New York: New York University Press.

Darling-Hammond, L. (2004). Standards, accountability, and school reform. *Teachers College Record, 106,* 1047–85.

Davis, P. (1982). *A report on the expenditures of Title I, PSEN, and general tax levy funds by the community school districts and the Division of High Schools.* New York: Board of Education of the City of New York, Office of Funded Programs.

Delpit, L. (1995). *Other people's children: Conflict in the classroom.* New York: New Press; W.W. Norton.

DeParle, J. (2005, September 4). What happens to a race deferred? *New York Times,* pp. 1, 4.

Dougherty, J. (2004). *More than one struggle: The evolution of black school reform in Milwaukee.* Chapel Hill: University of North Carolina Press.

Dreier, P. (2005). *ACORN and progressive politics in America.* Paper presented at the ACORN: Past, Present, and Prospects Conference, University of Connecticut, Hartford, CT, December 6–7, 2005.

Elmore, R. F. (2002). Unwanted intrusion. *Education Next, 2*(1), 29–35.

Elmore, R. F., & Burney, D. (1997). *School variation and systemic instructional improvement in Community School District #2, New York City.* Pittsburgh, PA: Institute for Learning, Learning Research and Development Center, University of Pittsburgh.

Elmore, R. F., & Burney, D. (1999). Investing in teacher learning: Staff development and instructional improvement. In L. Darling-Hammond & G. Sykes (Eds.), *Teaching as the learning profession: Handbook of policy and practice.* San Francisco: Jossey-Bass.

Esposito, J. (2005). District profile: Hamilton County (Tenn.) schools reaching achievement. *DA/District Administration,* retrieved October 6, 2005, from www.districtadministration.com

Faulkner, W. (1956, March 5). A Letter to the North. *Life,* pp. 51–52.

Feller, M. A. (1982). *The performing arts alternative school: Two case studies.* Unpublished doctoral dissertation, Columbia University Teachers College.

Fennimore, B. (2005). *Brown* and the failure of civic responsibility. *Teachers College Record* (*107*)9, 1905–1932.

Ferguson, R. F. (1998). Teacher expectations and the test score gap. In Jencks, C., & Phillips, M. (Eds.), *The black-white test score gap* (pp. 273–317). Washington, DC: Brookings Institution.

First year evaluation of the CC9 Lead Teacher Project. (2005). New York: Academy for Educational Development.

Fiske, E., & Ladd, H. (2000). When schools compete: A cautionary tale. In D. Ravitch (Ed.), *Left back: A century of failed school reform.* New York: Simon & Schuster.

Fiske, E., & Ladd, H. (2001). Lessons from New Zealand. In P. Peterson & D. Campbell (Eds.), *Charters, vouchers, and public education.* Washington, DC: Brookings Institution.

Fliegel, S., with MacGuire. J. (1993). *Miracle in East Harlem: The fight for choice in public education.* New York: Manhattan Institute.

Foster, M. (2005). *Case study: When we decide to do something, we can work together to get it done: Collaborating in Chattanooga to close the achievement gap.* Portland, OR: Grantmakers for Education.

Framework for Action: School Communities That Work. (n.d.) Retrieved October 18, 2005, from http://www.schoolcommunities.org/aboutus/framework.html

Fruchter, N., & Siegel, D. (2002). *Final report: Evaluation of the performance driven budgeting initiative of the New York City Board of Education (1997–2000).* New York: New York University, Institute for Education and Social Policy.

Fuller, H. (2000, March). *The continuing struggle of African Americans for the power to make real educational choices.* Paper presented at the second annual symposium on Educational Options for African Americans, Milwaukee, WI.

Gambone, M. A., Klem, A. M., Summers, J. A., Akey, T. M., & Sipe, C. L. (2004). *Turning the tide: The achievement of First Things First education reform in the Kansas City, Kansas, public school district.* Philadelphia: Youth Development Strategies.

Gandara, P. (1995). *Over the ivy walls: The educational mobility of low-income Chicanos.* Albany: State University of New York Press.

Gans, H. (1967). *The Levittowners.* New York: Pantheon.

Gering, S. (2005). Making a reform the work of the district. *Voices in Urban Education, 9,* 22–28.

Gilyard, K. (1991). *Voices of the self: A study of language competence.* Detroit, MI: Wayne State University Press.

Glennan, T., Jr. (1998). *New American schools after 6 years.* Santa Monica, CA: RAND.

Gold, E., Simon, E., & Brown, C. (2002). *Strong neighborhoods, strong schools: Successful community organizing for school reform.* Chicago: Cross City Campaign for Urban School Reform.

Gutmann, A. (1987). *Democratic education.* Princeton, NJ: Princeton University Press.

Hallett, A. (Ed.). (1995). *Reinventing central office: A primer for successful schools.* Chicago: Cross City Campaign for Urban School Reform.

Hanushek, E. (1989). The impact of differential expenditures on school performance. *Educational Researcher, 18*(4), 45–51.

Hanushek, E. (1994). *Making schools work: Improving performance and controlling costs.* Washington, DC: Brookings Institution.

Hanushek, E. (1996). School resources and student performance. In G. Burtless (Ed.), *Does money matter? The effect of school resources on student achievement and adult success* (pp. 43–73). Washington, DC: Brookings Institution.

Heath, S. B. (1983). *Ways with words: Language, life, and work in communities and classrooms.* Cambridge; New York: Cambridge University Press.

Hedges, L. V., & Greenwald, R. (1996). Have times changed? The relation between school resources and student performance. In G. Burtless (Ed.), *Does money matter? The effect of school resources on student achievement and adult success* (pp. 74–92). Washington, DC: Brookings Institution.

Hedges, L. V., Laine, R. D., & Greenwald, R. (1994). Does money matter: Meta-analysis of studies of the effects of differential school inputs on student outcomes. *Educational Researcher 23*(3), 5–14.

Henig, J. (1998). School choice outcomes. In S. Sugarman & F. Kemerer (Eds.), (1999), *School choice and social controversy: Politics, policy, and law.* Washington, DC: Brookings Institution.

Henig, J. (1999). Race and choice in Montgomery County, Maryland, magnet schools. *Teachers College Record 96,* 729–34.

Hill, P. (2001). What is public about public education? In T. Moe (Ed.), *A primer on America's schools* (pp. 235–316). Stanford, CA.: Stanford University, Hoover Institution Press.

Hilliard, A. (2003). No mystery: Closing the achievement gap between Africans and excellence. In T. Perry (Ed.), *Young, gifted, and black: Promoting high achievement among African-American students* (pp. 131–165). Boston: Beacon Press.

Hirschman, A. (1970). *Exit, voice, and loyalty: Responses to decline in firms, organizations, states.* Cambridge, MA: Harvard University Press.

Holt, M. (2000). *Not yet "free at last": The unfinished business of the civil rights movement: Our battle for school choice.* Oakland, CA: ICS Press.

Ingersoll, R. M. (2004). *Why do high poverty schools have difficulty staffing their classrooms with qualified teachers?* Washington, DC: Center for American Progress and Institute for America's Future.

Interview with Anthony Alvarado: Making schools work. (2005, October 5). Interview conducted by Hedrick Smith for a Public Broadcasting System special, *District-wide Reform.* Retrieved October 9, 2005, from www.pbs.org/makingschoolswork/dwr/ny/alvarado.html

Janofsky, M. (2005, July 31). A new hope for dreams suspended by segregation. *New York Times,* pp. 1, 14.

Kao, G., & Tienda, M. (1998). Educational aspirations among minority youth. *American Journal of Education, 106,* 349–384.

Katz, M. (1993). *The "underclass" debate: Views from history.* Princeton, NJ: Princeton University Press.

Kingsbury, G., Olson, A., Cronin, J., Hauser, C., & Hauser, R. (2003). *The state of state standards.* Portland, OR: Northwest Evaluation Association.

Kirp, D. L. (2002). *Almost home: America's love-hate relationship with community.* Princeton, NJ: Princeton University Press.

Klarman, M. (2004). *From Jim Crow to civil rights: The Supreme Court and the struggle for racial equality.* New York: Oxford University Press.

Kluger, R. (1975). *Simple justice: The history of* Brown v. Board of Education *and Black America's struggle for equality.* New York: Knopf.

Kohl, H. (1967). *36 children.* New York: New American Library.

Krueger, A., & Card, D. (1996). *School resources and student outcomes: An overview of the literature and new evidence from North and South Carolina.* NBER Working Paper No. 5708. *Journal of Economic Perspectives, 10,* 31–50.

Labov, W. (1970). *The study of nonstandard English.* Champlain, IL: National Council of Teachers of English.

Labov, W. (1972). *Language in the inner city: Studies in the black English vernacular.* Philadelphia: University of Pennsylvania Press.

Ladson-Billings, G. (1994). *The dreamkeepers: Successful teachers of African American children.* San Francisco: Jossey-Bass.

Ladson-Billings, G. (2004). Landing on the wrong note: The price we paid for *Brown. Educational Researcher 33*(7), 10.

Lankford, H., Loeb, S., & Wyckoff, J. (2002). Teacher sorting and the plight of urban schools. *Education Policy Analysis Archives 24*(1), 37–62.

Lee, S. J. (1996). *Unraveling the model minority stereotype: Listening to Asian American youth.* New York: Teachers College Press.

Lee, V., & Bryk, A. (1993). Science or policy? A review of the quantitative evidence in Chubb and Moe's *Politics, markets, and America's schools.* In E. Rasell & R. Rothstein (Eds.), *School choice: Examining the evidence* (pp. 185–208). Washington, DC: Economic Policy Institute.

Linn, R. (2003). Accountability: Responsibility and reasonable expectations. *Educational Researcher 32*(7), 3–13.

Linn, R. L. (2005). Conflicting demands of No Child Left Behind and state systems: Mixed messages about school performance. *Education Policy Analysis Archives, 13,* 1–17.

Lopez, E. (2003). *Transforming schools through community organizing: A research review.* Cambridge, MA: Harvard University, Harvard Graduate School of Education, Harvard Family Research Project.

Lubienski, C., & Lubienski, S. T. (2006). *Charter, private, public schools and academic achievement: New evidence from NAEP mathematics data.* New York: National Center for the Study of Privatization in Education.

Malen, B., Ogawa, T., & Kranz, J. (1990). What do we know about school-based management? A case study of the literature—a call for research. In W. Clune & J. Witte (Eds.), *Choice and control in American education, Vol. 2* (pp. 289–334). New York: Falmer.

Mediratta, K. (2004). *Constituents of change: Community organizations and public education reform.* New York: New York University, Institute for Education and Social Policy.

Mediratta, K., Fruchter, N., & Lewis, A. (2002). *Organizing for school reform: How communities are finding their voice and reclaiming their public schools.* New York: New York University, Institute for Education and Social Policy.

Mediratta, K., & Karp, J. (2003). *Parent power and urban school reform: The story of Mothers on the Move.* New York: New York University, Institute for Education and Social Policy.

National Center for Education Statistics. (2002). *Common core of data.* National public education financial survey, 2001–2002. Washington, DC: U.S. Department of Education.

National Center for Education Statistics. (2005). *The nation's report card: America's charter schools: Results from the NAEP Pilot Study* (NCES Publication No. 2005-456). Washington, DC: Author.

National Center for Education Statistics. (2006). "Longitudinal School District Fiscal-Nonfiscal File, Fiscal Years 1990 to 2000, Common Core of Data." Retrieved February 1, 2006, from http://nces.ed.gov/pubsearch/pubsinfo.asp?pubid=2005863

National Commission on Excellence in Education. (1983). *A nation at risk: The imperative for educational reform.* Retrieved October 15, 2005, from http://www.ed.gov/pubs/NatAtRisk/index.html

New York City Department of Education. (2005). *Annual school reports* (ASR). New York: Author.

Noguera, P. A. (2003). *City schools and the American dream: Reclaiming the promise of urban education*. New York: Teachers College Press.

Orfield, G., & Lee, C. (2005). *Why segregation matters: Poverty and educational inequality*. Cambridge, MA: Harvard University, The Civil Rights Project.

Perry, T. (2003). *Young, gifted, and black: Promoting high achievement among African-American students*. Boston: Beacon Press.

Putnam, R. (1995). Bowling alone: America's declining social capital. *Journal of Democracy 6*(1), 65–78.

Quint, J., Bloom, H. S., Black, A. R., & Stephens, L., with Akey, T. (2005). *The challenge of scaling up educational reform: Findings and lessons from First Things First. Final report*. New York: MDRC.

Reed, A., Jr. (1999). *Without justice for all: The new liberalism and our retreat from racial equality*. Boulder, CO: Westview Press.

Resnick, L. B. (2003, August 7). Reforms, research, and variability: A reply to Lois Weiner. *Education Policy Analysis Archives 11*(28). Retrieved November 21, 2005, from http://epaa.asu.edu/epaa/v11n28/.

Resnick, L., & Glennan, T. (2002). Leadership for learning: A theory of action for urban school districts. In A. Hightower, M. Knapp, J. Marsh, & M. McLaughlin (Eds.), *School districts and instructional renewal* (pp. 160–172). New York: Teachers College Press.

Romo, H. D., & Falbo, T. (1996). *Latino high school graduation: Defying the odds*. Austin: University of Texas Press.

Rothstein, R. (2004). *Class and schools: Using social, economic, and educational reform to close the black-white achievement gap*. Washington, DC: Economic Policy Institute; New York: Columbia University, Teachers College Press.

Roza, M., & Hawley Miles, K. (2002). *A new look at inequities in school funding: A presentation on the resource variations within districts*. Seattle, WA: Center on Reinventing Public Education.

Rubin, L. B. (1972). *Busing and backlash: White against white in a California school district*. Berkeley and Los Angeles: University of California Press.

Rury, J., & Mirel, J. (1997). The political economy of urban education. *Review of Research in Education 22*, 49–110.

Rustin, M. (2003, October). *Rethinking audit and inspection*. Paper presented at the third Tavistock Clinic Policy Seminar, London.

Ryan, J. E. (2004). The perverse incentives of the No Child Left Behind Act. *New York University Law Review, 79*, 932–989.

Saltman, K. (2005). *The Edison schools: Corporate schooling and the assault on public education*. New York: Routledge.

Schneider, M., Teske, P., & Marschall, M. (2000). *Choosing schools: Consumer choice and the quality of American schools*. Princeton and Oxford: Princeton University Press.

School Communities That Work: A National Task Force on the Future of Urban Districts. (2002). *School communities that work for results and equity*. Providence, RI: Brown University, Annenberg Institute for School Reform.

Self, R., & Sugrue, T. (2002). The power of place: Race, political economy, and identity in the postwar metropolis. In J. Agnew & R. Rosenzweig (Eds.), *A companion to post-1945 America* (pp. 20–43). Oxford: Blackwell.

Shirley, D. (1997). *Community organizing for urban school reform.* Austin: University of Texas Press.

Siddle Walker, V. (2001). African American teaching in the South: 1940–1960. *American Educational Research Journal, 38*(4), 769–771.

Smrekar, C., Guthrie, J. W., Owens, D. E., & Sims, P. G. (2001). *March toward excellence: School success and minority achievement in Department of Defense schools. A report to the National Education Goals Panel.* Nashville, TN: Vanderbilt University, Peabody Center for Education Policy.

Stanton-Salazar, R. (2001). *Manufacturing hope and despair: The school and kin support networks of U.S.-Mexican youth.* New York: Teachers College Press.

Stein, M. K., & D'Amico, L. (2002). The district as professional learning laboratory. In A. M. Hightower, M. S. Knapp, J. A. Marsh, & M. W. McLaughlin (Eds.), *School districts and professional renewal* (pp. 61–75). New York: Teachers College Press.

Suarez-Orosco, C., & Suarez-Orosco, M. (2001). *Children of immigration.* Cambridge, MA: Harvard University Press.

Sukstorf, M., Wells, A., & Crain, R. (1993). A re-examination of Chubb and Moe's *Politics, Markets, and America's Schools.* In E. Rasell & R. Rothstein (Eds.), (pp. 209–218). Washington, DC: Economic Policy Institute.

Sunstein, C. (2004, May 21). Did *Brown* matter? *The New Yorker,* pp. 102–107.

Talbott, M. (2004). Parents as school reformers. In A. Russo (Ed.), *School reform in Chicago.* Cambridge, MA: Harvard University Press.

Tierney, J. (2006, February 21). Let your people stay. *New York Times,* p. A19.

Tyack, D., & Cuban, L. (1996). *Tinkering toward utopia: A century of education reform.* Cambridge, MA: Harvard University Press.

Valenzuela, A. (1999). *Subtractive schooling: U.S.-Mexican youth and the politics of caring.* Albany: State University of New York Press.

Warren, M. (2001). *Dry bones ratting: Community building to revitalize American democracy.* Princeton, NJ: Princeton University Press.

Warren, M. (2005). Communities and schools: A new view of urban education reform. *Harvard Educational Review 75*(2), 133–173.

Weiner, L. (2003, August 7). Research or "cheerleading"? Scholarship on Community School District 2, New York City. *Education Policy Analysis Archives 11*(27). Retrieved November 21, 2005, from http://epaa.asu.edu/epaa/v11n27/

Wells, A. (1993). The sociology of school choice: Why some win and others lose in the educational marketplace. In E. Rasell & R. Rothstein (Eds.), *School choice: Examining the evidence* (pp. 29–48). Washington, DC: Economic Policy Institute.

Wells, A., & Crain, R. (1992). Do parents choose school quality or school status? A sociological theory of free market education. In P. Cookson (Ed.), *The choice controversy* (pp. 65–82). Newbury Park, CA: Corwin Press.

Wideman, J. E. (1984). *Brothers and keepers.* New York: Holt, Rinehart, Winston.

Wilentz, C. J. (1990). Abbott v. Burke, Supreme Court of New Jersey, 119 N.J. 287, decided June 5, 1990.

Wilson, T. A. (1996). *Reaching for a better standard: English school inspection and the dilemma of accountability for American public schools.* New York: Teachers College Press.

Witte, J. (2000). *The market approach to education: An analysis of America's first voucher program.* Princeton, NJ: Princeton University Press.

Young, B. A. (2003). *Characteristics of the 100 largest public elementary and secondary school districts in the United States: 2000–01.* Washington, DC: National Center for Educational Statistics. Retrieved October 15, 2005, from http://nces.ed.gov/Pubs2003/100_largest

Zachary, E., & olatoye, S. (2001). *Community organizing for school improvement in the South Bronx: A case study.* New York: New York University, Institute for Education and Social Policy.

Index

About the Author

NORM FRUCHTER is Director of the Community Involvement Program of the Annenberg Institute for School Reform at Brown University. For the past decade, he served as Director of New York University's Institute for Education and Social Policy and as a faculty member of NYU's Steinhardt School of Education. He was previously the Program Advisor for Education at the Aaron Diamond Foundation, a foundation committed to improving public education in New York City. He has also worked as a Senior Consultant with the Academy for Educational Development and Advocates for Children of New York and as Director of the Institute for Citizen Involvement in Education in New Jersey. He was the co-founder and co-director of Independence High School, in Newark, New Jersey, an alternative high school for drop-outs. For ten years he served as an elected school board member for Brooklyn's District 15. He is a co-author of *Hard Lessons: Public Schools and Privatization* (1996), *New Directions in Parent Involvement* (1992), and *Choosing Equality: The Case for Democratic Schooling* (1987). He has also authored two novels, *Coat Upon A Stick* (1963) and *Single File* (1970).